**pitch**

# pitch

## What to know, do and say
## to make the perfect pitch

Shaun Varga

**Prentice Hall**
is an imprint of

Harlow, England • London • New York • Boston • San Francisco • Toronto • Sydney • Singapore • Hong Kong
Tokyo • Seoul • Taipei • New Delhi • Cape Town • Madrid • Mexico City • Amsterdam • Munich • Paris • Milan

**PEARSON EDUCATION LIMITED**

Edinburgh Gate
Harlow CM20 2JE
Tel: +44 (0)1279 623623
Fax: +44 (0)1279 431059
Website: www.pearsoned.co.uk

First published in Great Britain in 2009

ISBN: 978-0-273-72511-4

*British Library Cataloguing-in-Publication Data*
A catalogue record for this book is available from the British Library

*Library of Congress Cataloging-in-Publication Data*
Varga, Shaun.
  Brilliant pitch : what to know, do and say to make the perfect pitch
  / Shaun Varga.
    p. cm.
  ISBN 978-0-273-72511-4 (pbk.)
  1. Sales presentations. 2. Selling. 3. Success in business. I. Title.
  HF5438.8.P74V37 2009
  658.8'101—dc22
                          2009029154

10 9 8 7 6 5 4 3 2 1
13 12 11 10 09

Typeset in 10/14pt Plantin by 3
Printed and bound in Great Britain by Henry Ling Ltd, Dorchester

The publisher's policy is to use paper manufactured from sustainable forests.

# Contents

# About the author

**Shaun Varga** is Chairman and Creative Director of Ingenuity, a new business development consultancy, which advises both marketing services agencies and sporting organisations on how to pitch for new business.

After an MA from Christ Church Oxford, Shaun began his career in 1986, joining advertising agency JWT London as an Account Executive. He has worked at senior levels in a wide range of marketing services agencies in the UK and Europe, including advertising, film and video, digital, design and public relations.

He has co-founded two creative agencies, including the digital agency Glue, and worked as Marketing Consultant to a government-funded business incubator.

In his spare time he is a keen yachtsman, motorcyclist and player of the Great Highland Bagpipe. He is married with one daughter and lives in Surrey.

# Acknowledgements

To my wonderful family; my wife Caroline and daughter Emily, thank you for putting up with me whilst writing this book.

I have had a great deal of help from friends and colleagues in the industry, especially in respect of the stories featured throughout the book. These include Jeremy Garner, Nick Gray, Bill Hart, Adam Kirby, John Lowery, Simon Marquis, Dominic O'Meara and Rick Sareen, in particular. Thank you also to all those people who preferred not to be mentioned individually! Finally, a special thanks to Andrew Wilder for his many words of wisdom and illustrative examples.

# Read this first

I'm not a big fan of 'introductions'. If you're like me, you probably skip them and get straight into the meat. But bear with me, this is important. Hence the title, 'Read this first'.

Why are *you* reading this book?

Many of the people who read *Brilliant Pitch* are doing so because pitching forms part of their job and, typically, a very obvious part at that. If you currently work in sales or marketing, or for a marketing or communications agency, then pitching is obviously a core skill you will need to master. No surprise there. But the truth is, there is almost no career that doesn't require an ability to put together and deliver an effective pitch from time to time. Moreover, when those times do occur, they tend to be at critical moments in the career path – getting that next big job, selling in a new initiative, defending a previous decision and so on. These are the times when, to use a phrase coined by US advertising agency Chiat/Day, 'good enough isn't good enough'.

The key to it all is simply this . . .

There is an acronym frequently used in the world of marketing – AIEDA. It stands for awareness, interest, evaluation, desire, action. It covers the typical steps in a typical purchase cycle. It has been around for years; you will find it in most marketing textbooks, along with its shorter sibling AIDA (some things, chocolate bars perhaps, don't require a lot of 'evaluation').

This book is based on the premise that, in pitching, this formula is flawed. Contrary to over 50 years of received wisdom, there is a better way.

The better way is the method I call IDEA.

The IDEA that underpins a brilliant pitch – as opposed to an average pitch – is that desire should be created *ahead* of evaluation and action. This simply reflects what I have gleaned from over 20 years in the world of marketing communications – the simple but crucial observation that most times, a prospect already knows what they want to buy *before* the day of the pitch. The logical consequence of this is that most pitch competitors walk into a situation in which they are already the option the prospect does *not* want to buy. Everything you are about to read is designed to help you ensure that you are not one of them.

And finally, in case you were wondering, all the stories you are about to read are, to the best of my knowledge, true.

# CHAPTER 1

# So how good are you … really?

Mapping yourself on the gradient of pitch gurudom, and why you're almost certainly better than you think.

You know how sometimes you meet somebody who is successful, wealthy, intelligent, articulate, at the pinnacle of their career, with the tan and the teeth to match? It's an easy assumption to make that this person would perform well in a pitch situation. I met a person exactly like that some years ago. With film star looks, a sharp intellect and the self-confidence that courses through the veins of those who already own a second home abroad, how could he possibly fail?

My company had been assisting in the marketing of his business (an advertising agency) and we had become concerned by the lack of conversion of pitch opportunities into paying clients. This agency had forgotten how to win. The most recent one was particularly galling. Kirk, the managing director (not his real name, but it should have been), sat at his desk looking particularly glum. 'So Kirk,' I say, 'why the long face?'

'We didn't get the XYZ pitch.'

'No way! I thought you said it was fantastic. What happened . . . ?'

'It was a brilliant pitch! The strategy was genius, the work was really original and fresh. Bill presented it spot on. And although I say it myself, I was fantastic, I mean really in the zone. Can't understand it – must have been fixed.'

And so we decided to find out what really went wrong. The

answer came through a simple 'post-pitch debrief' call to the prospect, who as it turned out was only too happy to tell all.

'The thinking was a bit predictable, the work was nothing special – I've seen that sort of thing plenty of times before – but the main thing was the people. They'd done no preparation about us, about me, about the market, and then they come in here acting like they know it all. And their MD was incredibly arrogant . . . ! They basically came last by a mile.'

Do you know what? I got the distinct impression that this prospect was delighted that I'd phoned, as he seemed to feel the need to get this off his chest. (There were a few expletives in there too, for added emphasis, which I've taken out.) He was *genuinely angry* that the pitch was so wide of the mark. This reaction is completely predictable. Herein lies the key to how we can ensure that your own pitching ends up brilliant and not just competent.

## Your audience wants you to succeed

I have found it to be the case, time and again, that the people to whom you are pitching are *genuinely* willing you to succeed. How great is that? They *want* you to be the answer to their problems – to their prayers even. Have you ever had the experience of interviewing people for a job, and you really need to find the right person, and you're hoping that every new interviewee might turn out to be that person? Trust me on this. When you're on the receiving end of a pitch there is nothing better than when someone makes your life easy – by making it easy for you to say yes.

> the people to whom you are pitching are genuinely willing you to succeed

If you're reading this then pitching will be important to you. Maybe it's because pitching is an important part of your job (you're in sales, perhaps). Or maybe you've never pitched before in your life, but now you need to and, consequently, you have one pitch in particular on your mind. In either case, you can take heart from the story above. The prospect was angry because it was really important to his business (possibly to his own personal career prospects) that someone pulled a brilliant pitch out of the bag. His stress levels were going up because he knew that given a pitch list of three, his chances of achieving his own objectives had just gone down by a third.

The fact that the desire for a successful outcome is shared equally by your audience is a key factor in developing a pitch. 'Brilliance' is not an absolute value, it is a relative one. Your audience will assist you in defining it, whether you like it or not.

## brilliant tip

Relax. Underneath the frosty exterior, your prospect will be secretly willing you to do really well. Because if you *don't*, they will be no further forward in finding a solution to their problems.

And what of Kirk? Well, Kirk made some obvious errors, yet although the mistakes may seem obvious, you'd be amazed how often they crop up in pitches. He doomed himself to failure the minute he decided that his experience and brilliance were such that he could short-cut the preparation. Fortunately for us all, the world is full of people like these – prospects who want you to win, and competitors who seem hell bent on losing, lacking either the knowledge or the inclination to produce a brilliant pitch.

## Great news! You already know how to pitch

Another encouraging fact is this. I referred to the person 'who has never pitched before' a couple of paragraphs back. This person simply does not exist. Everyone has pitched. By the age of ten, most children in mainstream social situations have learned important lessons in how to get their parents to agree to things. Take my daughter. She can manipulate me not because she has been on some sales course, but simply because she has picked up how to press exactly the right buttons to get me to act in the way she wants. Her approach may fall flat on someone else (wrong buttons), but it works on me every time.

brilliant pitching is very much a process of working out which buttons to press

Standard pitching is a lot about selling, but brilliant pitching is very much a process of working out which buttons to press by getting under the skin of your audience. It's a little like being a detective. Have you noticed how the comments people write in leaving cards for departing colleagues can be surprisingly funny and apt? Is it because there is a talented comedian hidden away in most people? No. It's because these comments are based on a very high – almost intimate – level of knowledge about the target audience. The more you know about your audience, the easier it gets.

## It's all about the IDEA

I'm going to make a radical suggestion to you: that whatever level you think you are at, by following my method it will be easier for you to produce a brilliant pitch than to produce a merely good pitch. A 'good' pitch will include a lot of stuff you can get from reading a book about sales and a book about presentation skills. It will therefore (by definition) be somewhat generic, and so it follows that it will probably be quite similar to the kind of pitch your competitors will produce. My method is designed to help you construct and deliver a compelling, competitive advantage for when you absolutely, definitely want to win. Its premise is that the old marketing 'purchase cycle' model known as AIEDA (awareness, interest, evaluation, desire, action) is flawed in a pitch situation, and that brilliant pitches are based on a new model: IDEA. In the IDEA pitching model, awareness is a given and the crucial shift is that desire now comes *before* evaluation and action. Most people don't get that. This is why *you* can be *brilliant*.

Many of the people I talk to suffer from anxiety about how good they are at pitching. 'I'm not a natural in front of an audience,' they'll tell me. What they mean is that they feel uncomfortable in front of an audience and under pressure. You may have given some thought as to where you yourself lie along the spectrum of pitch genius. Your conclusions might be causing you some concern. If they are, you are troubling yourself unnecessarily. Let's consider one highly relevant example of oratory. Bar-room oratory.

## Brilliant pitches are an everyday occurrence

If you want to hear some of the best (most effective) pitching, you might want to pop into a bar in any big city an hour or so after work. It's quite enlightening. What you will find are the middling ranks of the office-dwelling world letting off steam, putting the world to rights and also putting their own organis-ations to rights. The latter example is where it gets interesting. Very often I've overheard really outstandingly persuasive 'pitches' – one person putting forward a strong argument, without notes, props or any trace of nerves, which completely persuades their audience. I've often thought, 'Wow! That was good!' Followed by, 'If only you could do that during working hours rather than afterwards, you would be these people's boss not their colleague.' What I was tuning into were three elements, three vital lessons for anyone keen to improve their pitch per-formance. Let's examine each one in turn.

The first thing is passion.

## Be passionate

You can hear it in the voice, you can see it in the eyes, that right here, right now, this person cares more about this topic than anything else in the whole wide world. Not only that, but you'll also notice that they possess an absolute, unshakable conviction that they are right. This sheer conviction creates a powerful impression. An impression that can be so powerful that I have seen it carry the day on many occasions despite the merits of the case – sometimes even when the case being made is patently absurd. That's a powerful weapon. It's a weapon people find easy to deploy in a bar environment because they are at ease; they don't feel threatened, they know that in a bar they can speak more freely, they know their audience and they're not afraid of offending them.

> sheer conviction creates a powerful impression

Where they go wrong is that as soon as they walk into the office, they park all that at the door. Sadly, most offices contain lots of nervous people who seldom say what they really mean and always nod when asked if they agree with the consensus view. This kind of behaviour might, in the more disappointing variety of organisation, provide you with a long and successful career. But it's no way to act in a pitch. One sure way to make any buyer feel nervous about saying yes is to give them the sense that you're not completely sure that *you* would say yes. You cannot expect anyone to buy into a proposition unless it's crystal clear that you have 100 per cent belief in its validity.

You can also watch this technique in action around the world, in places like the House of Commons and the US House of Representatives. In politics, many fine careers have been established upon the solid rock of unswerving self-belief in the face of contradictory evidence. The surprising thing, of course, is that they keep on getting away with it. How does that happen? It happens for the simple reason that they are able to stand up and tell us with real passion and conviction that black is white. They don't just tell us this, they proclaim it! They explain that in this day and age no sane, reasonable and rational human being could possibly think otherwise – and so they *demand* that we believe it. And enough of us do to get them by. But these particular politicians share one other important characteristic with our bar-room pitch experts.

They know their subject. But only to a point.

## A little knowledge is a wonderful thing

We know that in the bar, the passion comes from the relaxed environment (and let's not forget that the passion will have been cranked up several notches now that the lager is kicking in . . .), but the conviction part actually comes from having a good grasp of the subject matter. So the brilliant pitches in the bar environment tend not to be the ones where the orator is picking holes in the CEO's explanation of the company's operational gearing.

> conviction comes from having a good grasp of the subject matter

Oh no. You can bet it'll be when it's about something that impinges upon the orator's own job. And we're all experts on our own job, aren't we?

Well, actually no, in fact we're not. There may be many factors that relate to our role about which we remain almost totally ignorant. Factors that might from another perspective completely outweigh our own narrow point of view. The point here is not that the bar-room orator knows everything about their job, but simply that they know enough about it. Enough to overwhelm the current audience. Did I mention politicians? Again, note that when politicians are talking about a topic, they will have absorbed not *every* fact connected with it, but just enough key facts to support their own standpoint, as well as a few to knock down the most likely opposing view. You do get some with a genuinely broad and deep grasp of their subject, but not often. Like a politician, you too could get by on a handful of 'need to know' facts, but only if you have thought through what is required in order to sustain your argument. Don't knock it. It works.

An extremely helpful phenomenon for any pitcher is the thing I call 'knowledge gap elasticity'. Say there are two people in the room, A and B, and they're discussing gardening. Early on, person A demonstrates slightly more knowledge about gardening than person B. At this point knowledge gap elasticity kicks in, because person B will now assume that person A knows a lot more about gardening than is actually the case. The more technical or academic the subject, the wider the knowledge gap will be assumed to be. I used to find this a lot when I ran digital marketing agencies. Because we actually *did* know more about digital issues than our clients, our opinion would always prevail. However, it was clear from talking to them that our clients had assumed we were gurus on the subject and absorbed what we had to say without question. If we'd wanted, we could have made up any old nonsense and they would have believed it. But that's because by then I knew just where the boundaries lay. I had my audience nailed. Not only did I know where the areas of ignorance were, I also knew what kind of suggestions they wanted to hear. I could already guess what the 'right answer' would be to most questions. And this brings us to the third and final point arising from bar-room oratory.

Bar-room orators don't pitch to strangers.

## Never pitch to a stranger

This is perhaps the least obvious but most significant point. Watch what happens next. The orator, without even fully appreciating the power of his knowledge, will pick off the audience one by one. He can do this because he knows exactly what buttons to press. He knows that Clive, for example, hates filling in forms and so he can emphasise how his own plan would halve the number of forms that need filling in. So Clive's nodding already. Judy, meanwhile, is a big fan of the bonus scheme because she relies on it to fund the school fees. The orator knows this too. So the next point is how his plan would improve sales performance and thus help the team beat the bonus by 50 per cent. Now Judy's nodding too, and believe me, collective agreement is a very contagious thing. Skilfully our orator has manipulated the needs and wants of his audience and got them onside straight away. And chances are he didn't even realise that what he was doing was creating desire *ahead* of evaluation and action. But we too could do this, and do so quite deliberately, if only we knew a bit more about our audiences. If only we didn't have to pitch to strangers.

### brilliant tip

The hardest person in the world to pitch to is a stranger. The most effective pitches happen when you are pitching not to a company or to a job title, but to a *person* you have already got to know.

So how good are you at pitching? Forget it, it doesn't matter. If you can understand how someone in a bar can win an argument through passion and self-belief, knowing the right things about a subject and the right things about an audience, then you are already on the way to being a better pitcher than you are now.

**CHAPTER 2**

# It's OK if you haven't done it before: the importance of clarity

Being clear about objectives, getting yourself in the right mindset and how to begin at the beginning.

'Be still, my beating heart!'

There are other ways to describe how it feels when you're suddenly in pitch mode. As it happens, 'Be still, my beating heart!' is the only one that made it past my publisher. But trust me, I know what that feeling is like. Oh yes. Personally, I enjoy it – I like the challenge, it excites me, it gets me into competitive mode and suddenly I feel like I have a defining task to complete. But that's just me. You may not be the same. Perhaps you didn't ask for the challenge in the first place (unwilling). Perhaps you find it a massively unwelcome departure from your comfort zone (uncertain). Perhaps you don't actually like pitching for things in any case (uncompetitive). In my experience, there is always a point where you're going to have to pitch to other people in order to get what you want, even if you're feeling unwilling, uncertain or uncompetitive. This might, in extreme cases, seem contrary to your entire belief system.

But you're stuck with it. So what now?

## Strength through joy

When you break the process down into bite-sized chunks (which you can, every time), it gets easier to see the way forward, and to see how the component parts all fit together. Once you can see that, you can relax. Relax and enjoy the ride . . .

Enjoyment plays a big part in doing things well. If you don't enjoy a particular thing, the chances are you won't be much good at it. Financial management, for example, is something I hate doing. There's absolutely no enjoyment there. And yet some people (admittedly some of the dullest I know) get a real kick out of being an accountant. I am however *capable* of tackling financial matters competently, and I have learned to find a strange pleasure in the emotional benefit of getting the job finished. When I've got my financial stuff organised, there's a sense of relief. When I was a student I spent a couple of months in Peru, travelling around on smelly, overcrowded trains, sitting next to chickens, sleeping in draughty rooms with random rodents in what passed for hotels high up in the Andes. This was most certainly 'roughing it', even by the standards of your average student. The return flight to England was with British Airways, and I tell you, walking into the aircraft was like someone had just turned civilisation back on, like you'd flicked a switch and turned the lights on. The second I sat down in my seat there was an overwhelming, visceral sense of relief. Nice clean plane, nice clean air stewardesses and the calm, reassuring voice of the captain (who must surely have been a voiceover artist on the side) mellowing over the intercom. Every fibre in my body, and mind, immediately began to relax. That's what finishing my domestic finances feels like. That's how I get through it. If I can do it, you can do it.

A good place to start any pitch is to focus on the ending. A happy ending. After all, English rugby player Jonny Wilkinson probably didn't actually enjoy the endless practice sessions, kicking ball after ball between the tall posts, in the dark and the rain. But I have an idea that somewhere in his mind was the emotional anticipation of the end product (famously, his extraordinary World Cup winning kick in the dying seconds of the game against Australia).

> a good place to start any pitch is to focus on the ending

## Being clear about objectives

The first question to ask yourself is this: why am I doing this pitch at all? What's in it for me? What's the upside of the victory? Whether it's winning a large order and generating equally large amounts of commission, or persuading someone to agree to see things your way, or just winning out of sheer bloody-mindedness, there's always something in it for you. Imagine the outcome going your way, and now imagine exactly how that's going to feel. Remember that feeling because it will be a great comfort to you during the pitch process. Like your own personal genie in a bottle, when things get tough (and they will) it's good to have a big, powerful, helpful thing waiting to be summoned up at a moment's notice. Focus on your happy ending and you can settle down to begin at the beginning. The beginning is to establish clarity about your objectives.

 **tip**

Be *clear* about your corporate and departmental objectives. But be *honest* about your own personal objectives. Are they aligned? If not, how do you propose to deal with it?

There are two kinds of objective in any pitch. There are the objectives that you tend to find written down on paper and there are the objectives that lurk inside your head. It's the ones inside your head that you need to tackle first. The more honest you are about these, the sooner we can start. I've been on pitch teams in the past where one or more members of the team have clearly had their own personal agenda. So 'fess up – is this about personal aggrandisement? Do you want to put one over on someone else, or shine in front of the boss, or even prove something to your spouse? We will return to this topic in more detail later in the chapter.

A helpful tool to assess this is the objectives cone. Imagine the wide base, the sharp point at the top. It's a cone split into four slices by three horizontal lines. There is room inside for all three interested parties: the company, the part of the company you belong to and you. The bottom segment of the cone is inhabited by the corporate objectives. Whether you work for a multinational conglomerate or run your own business, there will always be some big corporate goals that the organisation exists to achieve. They might even have told you what they are. Many businesses have objectives to do with being 'the leader' in something. The timeline for achieving these goals is usually a period of time longer than the duration of your pitch. Your pitch, in a small or perhaps large way, will fit into the corporate masterplan. The first reality check is that if it doesn't, then it shouldn't be happening. I've had this in my own businesses from time to time. We have been at the point of getting into a pitch process for something or other, then realised we were going into it for the wrong reasons – simply because we could, rather than because we *should*. We have usually pulled out and have never regretted any one of those decisions.

> your pitch will fit into the corporate masterplan

The next segment up is where your own departmental objectives lie. Let's just call it 'department level' for now, although it could as easily refer to a division, team, branch, store or aircraft carrier. This subcomponent will have its own part to play in achieving the corporate objectives. Hopefully, the two are aligned.

Now you might at this point be thinking, 'Where is he going with this? We're doing a pitch and the objective is simply to win, and winning is by definition aligned with every other objective.' This is, on the surface, a very plausible argument. But it is also flawed.

My company regularly takes client businesses through an induction process to get them 'pitch fit' for new business. It is designed to help us position them in the market and sell them in to prospects in exactly the right way. One of the things they have to do is step back and consider their corporate objectives. The objectives they come up with are never absolutes (although they often treat them as though they are). In reality, objectives exist somewhere along a dimension of possibility. 'Win new clients' is not an absolute. Are you saying you want to be market leader or just twice the size you are now? Over what period? Are we talking about two or three very large clients, or maybe 30 or 40 much smaller clients? Perhaps we're only interested in new clients prepared to pay retainer fees, or are we chasing clients that pay on a project basis? It's actually rather complicated, and the answers not only dictate the shape of the prospecting strategy that probably got you to the pitch stage in the first place, but should also dictate how you approach the pitch itself.

## Consider the cost of victory

A commonly used corporate rallying cry, especially in a downturn, is 'let's not be afraid to win ugly'. The implication is that winning is everything and that anything else is secondary. The truth of it is that this is an invitation to make compromises compared to your normal behaviour. Any organisation needs to think very carefully about what compromises it makes. Does it mean that the corporate objective is suddenly 'win at any cost'? I don't think that is ever truly the intention, but again, it's all a matter of degree. If you pitch a lower price than normal, how far down do you go? More importantly, what compromise is going to be made in order to fund the reduction? The compromises you make will, at some point, have an impact on your customers. If winning ugly means winning unprofitably, you might go bust and that could cause a big problem for both you and your customers. If you compromise on service levels or product quality, the impact on the customer is obvious and will inevitably come home to roost. You may not get a second chance to pitch.

 **tip**

'Winning ugly' should never be misunderstood to mean 'winning unprofitably' or in a way that will have an adverse impact on the longer-term health of the business.

In my current business, we never ever compete on price. We would rather lose. In fact, we are rather proud of the fact that we only lose pitches on price. Furthermore, we go out of our way to tell people when we've lost, and (perhaps counter-intuitively) this is a great new business asset. This is because our corporate objectives are focused on quality first, growth second, as we believe that offering the best quality on the market will deliver growth in any case. Our reputation is central to our entire strategy. There are many businesses in many fields that share a similar view. This has an interesting impact on pitches, because it shows how corporate objectives can lead you to behave in ways that seem like madness to people whose only agenda is to 'win the pitch' (ugly or otherwise). You might choose to conduct the pitch as though it were simply a stage on the road to the *next* pitch – the one where you win, and win beautifully. This is worthy of consideration. It takes the pressure off you emotionally (and that extra bit of objectivity that you will seem to bring to the pitch is an attractive quality). It's a strategy that also – helpfully – forces you to construct your argument very much from the point of view of the customer and the consequences of the decision they are about to make. You will invite them to consider their own personal position at varying stages in the future – six months, twelve months, two years, perhaps beyond. You will point out the impact this decision will have on other people (their bosses, colleagues, shareholders and so on). You will pose hypothetical questions and you will suggest questions their own board might ask in the event that, as you are predicting, X, Y and Z go wrong. It will be at the point where they start exchanging glances between themselves, possibly squirming on their seats a little, that you will know that you might, just might, get the gig first time round after all. It does happen!

But back to the cone.

## Personal versus professional objectives

Next stage up, as the cone gets thinner above departmental level 2, are levels 3 and 4. Both of these are for you. There's a reason why you get to have two levels rather than one. The first category is for you in your professional capacity as an employee of your company, while the second is for you in your capacity as, well, you. And guess what? They're not necessarily the same. In fact they can be completely contradictory.

Consider the pitch (it's an extreme, but real, example) in which a relatively junior female team member was given a clear and simple task, namely to ensure that the travel logistics were such that everyone, including her, would get to the pitch on time, without fail. After careful consideration she made arrangements for three team members – herself, the team leader and the strategy guy – to stay at a nearby hotel. She had done this because her own personal objective was rather different – it was to sleep with the team leader. Now, having personal goals is fine, as any life coach will tell you, but this personal goal was so powerfully etched upon her soul that nothing was going to get in the way, certainly nothing as insignificant as a pitch. The strategy guy was there as camouflage, to make the arrangement seem less suspicious to other colleagues. Suffice it to say that one thing led to another, and the team leader got no sleep that night. On the day he didn't perform as well as he could have done, as he'd already performed better than he'd ever hoped the night before.

That's what happens to businesses when their people's objectives are not compatible with the company's objectives.

Hopefully your own personal objectives are consistent with your job title. Just like the corporate objectives, however, these too will involve some sort of balancing act along an axis – for example, thinker versus doer, leader versus follower. Or perhaps a scale that has 'individual brilliance' at one end and 'solid team player' at the other. Some people aspire to be seen as heroes, mavericks, rainmakers; the sort of people who can get away with certain defects because of the value of their strengths. This is not the norm, and there are not many examples of this working in the real world. Most people need to have a level of competence across a much broader range of skills. The pitch situation is, however, one of the few environments in which you can exist for a long time as a flawed hero. A senior planning director of a large London advertising agency got by for years on the strength of his sheer brilliance when it really counted, despite the fact that most of the time he just couldn't get himself motivated to do very much at all. When I was running creative agencies we used to say that the difference between an amateur creative team and a professional team was that given a deadline, the amateurs might come up with something brilliant but would probably come up with nothing. But the professionals would probably come up with something brilliant – and whatever happened, they would always come up with *something*. Something perfectly sellable. If you are capable of being occasionally brilliant you are capable of upping your consistency, just like anyone else.

## You can lose a battle and still win the war

A further potential similarity between personal and corporate objectives is that both may choose to play a longer game, seeing the pitch as a stepping stone to something better. Ultimately, you must make your own choices about what you have to gain from the pitch. Pitches are often an opportunity to impress, as there can be a great deal of attention being paid to their progress and their outcome within your organisation. So whatever happens, if you do your bit right you can achieve your objectives even in a losing situation. I knew someone once who was on a pitch team and lost, and she was absolutely delighted about it because she knew it was her boss's last-chance saloon. Her boss got fired and she got his job. An outstanding result for her. One thing she had made a point of doing throughout the pitch was to be seen to be always the first volunteer to step forward, seen to be seeking and taking responsibility, going the extra mile, helping her colleagues. The operative word here being 'seen'. Her other master stroke was to have spotted that the ultimate decision maker regarding the internal job was a man who relied heavily on his personal assistant. It was a simple task to then use the PA, subtly and cleverly, as a conduit to ensure the decision maker's perception of events was skewed in her favour. This may not be the most desirable situation when looking at it with a corporate hat on, and most corporate organisations would not recognise the validity of your own personal segment of my objectives cone. I tell you this because one of the principles of this book is the importance of focusing on your audience, and I bet it wasn't your company that bought this book – I'll bet it was you.

> you can achieve your objectives even in a losing situation

# CHAPTER 3

# Basic mistakes: ever seen *Dragons' Den*?

The most common pitfalls and how to avoid them. Eliminating these will make an immediate improvement in your performance.

The TV programme *Dragons' Den* is, for those who may not have seen it, an opportunity for budding entrepreneurs to pitch their business ideas to a panel of millionaire entrepreneurs in the hope of gaining investment. Like most 'reality TV' shows, the true entertainment value lies in the fact that every week, two or three of the pitches will be absolutely, hilariously, disastrous. Even better, the reasons behind the hilarity are in almost all cases not only predictable, but also avoidable.

## Poor preparation

Some are obvious. Poor preparation is common. Time after time, the entrepreneurs are taken by surprise by the most obvious of questions. If you struggle with a really obvious question, it immediately sends out all kinds of warning signals and you will have to perform twice as well to recover. Any pitcher needs to be on top of their material. You need to know about you, your customers and about your competitors too. Any pitcher needs to understand the difference between features and benefits – benefits are what people buy, the features are just the means to an end. Most problems can be avoided by preparation.

**brilliant** tip

You can deliver a brilliant presentation and get away with style over substance. Unfortunately, not getting the substance right is simply not an option if you want to deliver a brilliant pitch.

The failed product demonstration is an old favourite. I particularly enjoyed the electric boiled egg cooking device that produced a few tepid, liquid eggs before its designer ran out of eggs (thus failing to prove that the contraption actually worked). He hadn't checked the thermostat.

*if anything* can *go wrong with the technical 'aids', it will*

The first rule of pitching is that if anything *can* go wrong with the technical 'aids', it will. Like any time you have to plug anything into some sort of display. If I had a pound for every time I'd heard the phrase 'OK, better get IT on the phone', I'd be a wealthy man. Not as rich as if I had a pound for every time IT took more than ten minutes to fix the problem.

The solution to this is to plan ahead, make sure that the person who actually knows how the kit works will be around *at the pitch* and do everything you can to ensure you are in the room, ready to set up, with an hour to go. Why an hour? Because although nine times out of ten everything will work well, when things do go wrong it will take at least half an hour for the guy with the strange hair and the Def Leppard T-shirt to fix it. It's a rule. Which still gives you half an hour to calm down and recover your composure before the pitch proper. Turning up well ahead of the start time is always good practice. It means you have time to compose yourself and avoid the hot flushes and other unwelcome symptoms exhibited by someone who's only just made it in time. I had someone pitch to me recently and remember trying to concentrate on the important message he was trying to convey, but failing. I couldn't take my eyes off the wet patches under each of his arms, as the dark shapes slowly grew ever larger. Pale blue shirts are bad for this – white is much better at disguising stress-induced sweat bloom.

## Make your first impression ... impressive

Another lesson we can learn from *Dragons' Den* is the importance of first impressions. It's scary how frequently you can predict, based on looks alone, which of the contestants will turn out to be the hilarious disasters. How you dress is far more significant than it should be. Nick Gray, Managing Director of specialist retail marketing agency Live & Breathe, told me about a pitch he'd once walked into. He and his colleagues had come well prepared – as they knew they needed to be, for this was a large and potentially valuable client they were chasing. So he gets out of the lift, just as one of the competitor companies is leaving. 'I felt like we'd lost it already,' he says, 'because they looked great!' Not a good start. He hadn't even got into the room at this stage. In front of him were four immaculately turned out opponents. 'I thought they looked every bit like exactly the kind of people you'd want looking after your business.'

One-nil to his opponents already. If one of their objectives had been to position themselves as exactly the right people to look after this business – and it almost certainly was – then they'd gone a long way down that track just by getting the right stuff out of the wardrobe that morning. Nick, meanwhile, had been put on the back foot straight away. Who knows what effect it had on the people they were pitching to. The opponents did win, by the way.

I spend a lot of time being pitched to in recruitment interviews. You'd be amazed at the state of some of the people who, while brilliantly well qualified on paper, put themselves at a huge disadvantage to the other interviewees. Some turn up looking like they've been in a train crash. Mainly, they turn up in the 'wrong' clothes. Nobody in my company wears a suit. Nobody in my industry wears a suit. So why do interviewees turn up wearing a suit? They could just randomly pick up a phone to anyone who works here and ask what people wear. And then they could turn up already looking like 'one of us', not like someone who works in the bank across the street.

## Clothes are a communication tool

your pitch clothes are your plumage

Your pitch clothes are your plumage, which means their primary purpose is communication. One company had a 'Meet the Directors' pro-gramme. Each major account manager would take one of their directors in to meet one of the customer's directors once a year to review their performance. The company was very strict about the dress code of its employees – dark suit, white shirt, sober tie, polished shoes. On one particular visit the account manager wore a blue suit, a pale blue shirt and a flowery tie. In the taxi on the way to the meeting his director spent the whole trip telling him off for wearing 'inappropriate' dress. On being shown into the customer's office the host was wearing literally the same suit, shirt and tie. They laughed at the coincidence and the meeting continued in the same relaxed manner. On the way back in the taxi the director spent the whole journey apologising for the telling off. He said that the account manager was right to dress for the customer environment and that the meeting had been more relaxed and successful because of it. Quite right too.

A former client of mine was told by his bosses at IBM that he should dress in such a way as to make the sales prospect feel comfortable. It seems to me that a lot of people used to interpret this as 'don't wear anything at all out of the ordinary'. But being ordinary is not the way to win a pitch. Clothes are a communication tool – so use it! If it is clear that you make an effort about your appearance, people will automatically assume you have high personal standards, take pride in yourself and your work and are generally switched on and buttoned down. But one note of caution: wearing a suit is not in itself a sign of taking pride in your appearance. In fact it can be quite the opposite. The standard 'office suit' is actually a very *lazy* way to dress. It's the default option, and therefore it communicates not effort, but the lack of it. If you haven't got, or can't afford, a 'super suit' then just invest some money in a very good shirt and designer accessories (cufflinks, tie, watch and so on). It will transform your appearance straight away.

**brilliant** tip

Like plumage, clothes are very important in most forms of courtship. Pitching is a form of courtship and clothes are a form of plumage. Unlike birds, you get to choose your own plumage.

Having established that clothes are a communication tool, what exactly is it that you need to communicate to your audience? Think hard about this. I have two job titles on my business card: Chairman and Creative Director. I need to dress differently depending on which hat I'm wearing. The reason is that the people I meet in either capacity come with a very different set of expectations and requirements. A chairman talking to an investor needs to be sensitive to the fact that investors are hugely reassured when the figurehead of the business looks cool, calm, in control and 'successful'. A CEO friend of mine spends a fortune on high-quality suits and shirts, as well as on a service that ensures a constant supply of clean, immaculately pressed shirts. Vanity? Certainly not. It is simply a calculated investment in his own career – an investment that, as he will tell you, has paid off handsomely. The thing that you are trying to sell may well be of deep importance to the buyer, and the more it matters to them the more you need to use every weapon in the armoury to reassure them of your ability to deliver.

Then, of course, there is the issue of your personal looks. Not everyone has been blessed with film star looks, and some of us look like we've been hit with the ugly stick. Have you seen those 'reality TV' makeover shows? Much as I detest reality TV, these shows do have a use in pointing out how easy it is to change. A good haircut is a good start, so cancel your next dinner out and invest the cash in a visit to the best hair stylist in town. When you walk out of the door in the morning looking – and feeling – great, you will find that your performance in the pitch will be the better for it.

## Take control of the agenda

Now you look the part, you can avoid the other common faults. Most of these will be eliminated by following the process contained in this book. However, on the day, in the pitch itself, things can happen that are difficult to deal with. With a little preparation these too can be overcome. It's interesting to study what it is about 'great pitchers' that makes them great. People who are consistently good at winning pitches have one thing in common – their ability to take control of the agenda.

I have been lucky enough to work with and learn from some outstanding individuals. My first board level boss at advertising agency JWT was a man named Andrew Brown, who went on to become Director General of the Advertising Association. Many's the time I saw him snatch victory from the jaws of defeat in client pitches, and frequently he did it by giving the client a new way of looking at an issue – one that fitted perfectly with our proposed solution. He is also the person who taught me a phrase I have found invaluable: 'Never let it be said that we can't take "Yes" for an answer'. In a pitch it's good to know when you have crossed the finishing line. Some sales courses will advise you to 'close hard and close often'. This is bad advice. Better to pay attention, be patient, spot the one perfect opportunity to close and *then* close hard. You'll find it an awful lot easier.

It is also useful to keep your antennae fully functional during the pitch (rather than switching into 'presenting' mode), because if you can pick up that your audience are not buying your pitch early enough, you can throw away the script and work with the buyer to re-engineer your approach. I have seen this technique work too, and it's infinitely preferable to flogging a dead horse just to fill the time.

### brilliant tip

One of the symptoms of brilliance – the ability to turn seeming defeat into victory – is frequently achieved by showing the prospect an entirely new way of looking at things. This is a skill that can be learned.

This ability to shape the outcome of a pitch (and I've seen it happen in a single sentence) is partly something that comes with experience and is partly mental agility. Mental agility is something you can practise. You can improve. If you played sport professionally, you wouldn't go into a big game without practising your core skills, would you? As a Manchester United fan, I recall the hours and hours David Beckham used to spend practising free kicks, and I also recall the gasps of amazement from commentators whenever he slotted in a goal from some impossible angle (something that happened quite regularly). The two things are connected – excellence requires practise.

## Give your brain a workout

Here are two exercises you can do that will help. The first is called 'Defend the Indefensible'. It does what it says on the tin; it's a game you can play with as many friends as you like. One of them will give you something 'indefensible' to defend in open debate. Stay away from 'lazy' topics (Hitler, for example) and get them to come up with things that are contemporary and preferably business related. You could try something like, 'Public transport should be abolished and everyone should have a car.'

The exercise of defending the seemingly indefensible relies on your ability to change the agenda, and sharpens up that ability very effectively. If you stick to the obvious agenda – the one clearly implied by the subject matter – you won't win. You will need to employ some lateral thinking to get anywhere. You will also need to think on your feet very quickly and consider what parts of your argument you put forward at what stage. If you say too much up front, you might restrict your room for manoeuvre and end up backed into a corner. This is one instance where being 'economical with the truth' can be a positive thing. You would therefore encourage your audience to put forward their objections early, so you can establish who has what sort of concerns. So, in the case of car versus public transport, you could choose from a hierarchy of defences, and might put them forward in reverse order, each one more persuasive than the last. These would probably include our old favourites, 'personal freedom' and 'the greater good'. For those who can't drive, your audience would dictate how you respond – you could choose to brush them aside (if they're up

*you will need to employ some lateral thinking to get anywhere* for the greater good argument) or give them a chauffeur (to appear concerned and caring if you're faced with an audience of social workers). All of the above skills are very relevant to anyone who wants to deliver a brilliant pitch.

I learned another useful exercise years ago, at school. One of the teachers, who had trained as a lawyer, claimed that as an advocate it was possible to construct a convincing argument, about anything, even when wholly unprepared. Quite a claim! He then went on to demonstrate. This exercise is called 'The solution to the world's problems'.

He invited the class to name anything and would argue that it was the solution to the world's problems. 'Taxis' were one suggestion, and he went with that. Half an hour later he had the lot of us sitting there seriously considering the idea that the taxi could indeed be the solution to the problems of the world. So how did he achieve that? As in the previous exercise, changing the agenda was a key tactic.

## Playing to your strengths

The first step is to redefine the issue at hand to play to your own strengths. This open-ended agenda ('the world's problems') gives you the opportunity to frame your own diagnosis of what those

> redefine the issue at hand to play to your own strengths

problems are at the outset and set the scene for a solution that only you can provide. In a pitch scenario, we frequently come across open-ended issues such as, 'How do we increase our sales?' This enables you to redefine the question early on, in your favour. In the marketing world this kind of question is manipulated routinely by marketing agencies. An advertising agency might argue that the true foundation of increased sales is to create a strong brand, reassuring to existing customers, attractive to new ones and resistant to competitive pressures like price (as people frequently pick the brand they know and like over a cheaper, but probably equally effective, alternative). On the other hand, a direct marketing agency might disagree, arguing that a highly personalised, targeted approach is what's needed, as this can deliver the right mix of messaging to a variety of audiences – and also provide a feedback loop for a 'test and refine' optimisation process. But then a 'shopper marketing' agency (yes, they do exist) might put forward a third alternative, based on the premise that a high percentage of purchase decisions are made at the point of sale. Therefore, they might argue, the thing to do is to focus your investment on the last few yards of the purchase process (literally) to ensure your product ends up in the shopping basket and not on the shelf.

There is merit in each approach, but the client has to choose. And in reality, the client will choose not simply on the basis of which approach they think will best increase their sales. In the real world, their choice may be based on a slightly different agenda. What's running through their heads at this point will be other considerations, just under the surface. Considerations such as, 'Can I measure the contribution of this particular activity accurately enough to justify my decision?' or, 'Which approach will be best at improving sales penetration amongst brand new customers?' or, 'Which will deliver the greatest return on investment?'

There's a key lesson in this. When you are in the business of selling hammers, every problem looks like a nail, and so your answers to questions tend always to be predictable and frequently wrong. I would suggest that, in the above example, the winner will be the competitor that is best aligned with all those key decision-making criteria that do *not* appear on the brief. The winner may get lucky and stumble across what they are. Or, you can redefine the issue at hand to play to your own strengths. You can give yourself a head start by knowing what buttons to press in order to generate desire prior to evaluation and action. That might require some mental agility, but then you are probably trying to achieve something a little more ambitious than selling an electric boiled egg cooking device.

# CHAPTER 4

# How not to make assumptions: finding out what they really want

It's not what you put into a pitch – it's what your audience takes out that matters. How to establish the criteria for success.

A recurring theme in this book is that there's someone else out there that you need to bring in at this very early stage. It's the person (or persons) to whom you are pitching. They too will have something to gain from the outcome of the pitch. This is the source of the desire you hope to create. You just need to find out, very precisely, what it is. This chapter is about how to check out the individuals on the buying team, and what you can infer from their professional behaviour to date.

Part of my work involves assessing 'lost pitches' on behalf of clients, during which I get to hear at first hand from the buyers how they think the pitch went and why they made their decision. When I started doing these, I used to think that most pitch decisions would be difficult ones, with strong competitors going head to head with little to choose between them. I was half right. In a pitch involving four or five competitors, it tends to be extremely easy to eliminate two or three straight away. Sometimes there's some debate about who the winner should be, and sometimes one competitor comes a very close second. But the thing that surprised me most was just how simple it is for buyers to rule out the majority of pitch contestants. Most pitch contestants don't merely lose, they miss by a mile. It happens all the time.

## Demonstrate an interest in your customer, not in yourself

A pitch criticism I've heard in various guises many times is, 'They were brilliant when it came to talking about themselves, but I can hardly remember them asking anything about me.' Perhaps that's

the hero of any pitch should be the customer

a failing that is particular to advertising agencies, but I suspect not. I think it's just more amplified in an advertising pitch. The hero of any pitch should be the customer. Not you. This applies even when you don't have a lot of time to make your pitch. My company runs business-to-business 'speed pitching' events, which bring together buyers and sellers in the creative industries. The feedback from these events matches the feedback from our pitch debrief work. The most common complaint is that those doing the pitching have got the wrong end of the stick in terms of understanding the buyer's real requirements. This means the pitchers have jumped to conclusions (probably the default conclusions they normally jump to – see the section on cognitive dissonance on page 97), haven't listened properly and/or didn't ask enough of the right questions in the first place.

At our 'speed pitching' events, the agencies doing the pitching tend to fall into two main camps. Each pitch session lasts precisely 11 minutes, and the first camp is comprised of those who see it as an opportunity to download as much information about themselves as they possibly can within those 11 minutes. These are the ones who tend to get a red light in our traffic-light rating system. The explanatory comments from the buyers are usually fairly scathing – they really do not like having to spend time (even 11 minutes of it) in the company of human brochureware. One buyer put her point of view to me rather memorably after one event: 'If I wanted to waste time listening to some muppet read out the standard flannel, I could go and sit in a conference. If these people aren't bright enough to take the opportunity to discuss what (company name) are looking for, I mean specifically, then I'm sorry but they're too stupid to be working with us anyway.' Well said! Who said pitching was supposed to be a one-way means of communication?

## brilliant tip

Any meeting in a pitch process is an opportunity *first* for you to find out about your prospect – and for them to find out about you *second*.

In the other camp are the people who view the 11 minutes as 11 minutes of cross-examination time. The most successful agencies at our events – according to the people they pitch to – are those that, after a very quick heads-up on who they are and what they do, get straight into a discussion about the buyers' current situation, needs, preferences, preferred way of working and so on. Only in the last few minutes do they begin to talk about how they propose to address these issues, in a very specific way, probably referring to a few success stories that will now be directly relevant to what has been discussed. The highly specific nature of this final stage of the session whets the appetite of the buyers (who are now hearing exactly the kind of thing they wanted to hear). They are already beginning to feel the desire. The session ends with them agreeing to continue the conversation separately, as soon as a slot can be found in their diaries. A brilliant result. Intelligent questioning and intelligent listening enable the seller to work out *exactly* what to say to the buyer to move the pitch process on to the next stage.

## The customer is not always right – and sometimes they lie

It therefore follows that you need to consider what it is that your buyers want and how you are going to make them a hero. Making your buyer a hero is never a bad strategy. The problem is that they often make it hard for you to find out what the real criteria for success are. What they say initially or in the brief may not represent the full truth. It may be incomplete; it may contain assumptions and conclusions that don't stack up.

A useful way to deal with this comes from the world of academia. People often ask how an MA in history from Oxford is at all relevant to a career in advertising. What, they ask, has history got to do with anything? At which point I argue that, in addition to the inherent value of the study of history (don't get me started!), it teaches you a method of thinking that is highly relevant to pitching. It all starts with a question that you have to answer. You go to your sources and examine the evidence, aiming off for any inbuilt bias. You then construct an argument of your own and repurpose the evidence to back up your own thesis. Finally, you have to defend your point of view in a one-on-one tutorial. Just like a pitch. It starts, as I said, with a question.

## Assumptions are there to be challenged

questions posed by buyers usually generate choices

Just as in the study of history, questions posed by buyers usually generate choices. A history question, such as 'Explain the reasons behind the breakdown of the political system in England between 1638 and 1642', opens up options; do you accept the premise of the question (that the political system *did* break down – and did so between those years), or do you challenge it, either on the basis of degree or timing?

In business, here is a real example that follows exactly this model. The founder of a food manufacturing business gave an interview to one of the popular business magazines. He was asked what professional regrets he had. His answer was that he regretted not being able to grow the business quickly enough to invest in advertising and thus build a bigger and more successful brand. A small comment containing a big assumption – that in order to build a successful brand you have to invest in advertising, and invest heavily. If you were pitching to him in connection with marketing communications, you would have to make a choice. Do you accept his view that a big advertising campaign *is* the key to building his brand? Or, conversely, do you point out that there are plenty of examples of successful brands, both national and global, which have been built via means other than advertising? You could argue that although he *thinks* he wants to be able to run a big advertising campaign, what he actually needs (to build a bigger and more successful brand) is something completely different. It would be wise to establish that before the pitch.

## Acquiring evidence

Depending on your level of access, the obvious thing to do is to quiz the prospect as thoroughly as possible on every aspect of the brief, including the most basic of assumptions. Leave no stone unturned, and don't be afraid to ask questions to which the answers seem obvious. The next level of research is where you switch into 'historian' mode and interrogate the sources. Your targets may have written things themselves. From authoring a major report to one of those 'day in the life' features in their staff magazine, there could be something useful there. I turned up to a pitch once on a motorcycle, knowing full well (thanks to a piece in his company's staff magazine) that the prospect was a motorcycle nut. Your targets may also have had things written about them. Go through press archives. Reports of job moves within the trade press are very useful. The typical format is:

*David Brent has been appointed head of marketing at Rainbow Box and Carton. He will be working alongside the CEO to develop new product areas. He joins after 18 months at Happy Valley Cardboard, where he trebled sales of Happy Landings Toilet Tissue through a controversial discounting policy.*

These articles tell us a lot. The information about where people have come from, what they did and why they left give us clues as to how they might react in various situations. David Brent is ambitious (as his short but successful tenure at HVC indicates), he now has a new product development brief and he's not scared of rocking the boat. When pitching to him, we would adjust the volume up and down in a very different way from if we were pitching to someone who had a track record of erring on the side of caution.

the career path of senior targets is very useful to know

Erring on the side of caution tends to be a feature of CEOs who have moved into that role via the finance director/CFO route. The career path of senior targets is very useful to know, whether or not you are pitching directly to them. Corporate culture and attitudes tend to disseminate down from the top. A cautious CEO breeds caution in the lower ranks. A real go-getter of a CEO, who was a useful amateur boxer in his younger days, is more likely to build a culture that is more aggressive and willing to take calculated risks. The pitch to these two organisations would be very different.

Social networking sources can be useful. LinkedIn, for example, is interesting for the people your target is linked to. Who are they, what do they do and what are they like? If your target has been endorsed or recommended, there will be an explanation of why that person is being endorsed and what characteristics are being acknowledged. As the study of history tells us, most sources contain some sort of bias. Anything written by anyone in PR can be assumed to be dripping with bias. It's their job. Anything written by someone who is junior to your target, such as a recommendation in LinkedIn, can also be assumed to be thoroughly self-serving. It might, however, tell us how our targets *like* to have themselves reported.

Your best, most accurate and up-to-date view of a prospect will come from someone who currently works with your target as a supplier or partner. It should be easy enough to discover other companies working alongside your prospect, and there's no reason why you can't talk to them. It's a little like a reverse interview situation, in which the interviewee is checking the references of the interviewer. You could explain that you are in discussion with your prospect, you're doing a bit of due diligence of your own and just want to check that they deal with their suppliers in a reputable way. The answer will probably be yes and then, as a throw-away line you can ask the real question: 'So do you know Mark Squires then? Oh really! What's he like?'

## Context matters – because people are different

Having gathered your contextual information about the individuals you are going to be facing off against, you can begin to build your argument. It may already be becoming clear whether you will couch your arguments in the language of seizing opportunities, stealing a march over competitors, taking a bold leap forward. Or whether perhaps it will be better to emphasise that your solution is the risk-free choice, delivering a solid and predictable result executed by a company famed as being the ultimate safe pair of hands. I say this because it doesn't always occur to people to actually use this kind of contextual information, even when they've got it.

**brilliant** tip

It's not always clear what to do with information you have discovered, because it opens up alternative ways forward. It is the contextual information that helps narrow the options down again.

I reviewed our outsourced IT suppliers not long ago. I spoke to three or four candidate suppliers, and in each case spent some time outlining our current situation – the kit, the software, the reasons why we were considering switching supplier and the kind of solution that would work best for us. I gave them this information because I wanted to make life easy for them, and in turn for me – as I would have four sets of proposals to choose from, each one of which would be spot on in terms of matching my requirements. Two of them came back with a completely standard, menu-based proposal with one piece of personalisation – someone had cut and pasted our logo on to the cover page. Straight in the bin. The third had managed to include an opening paragraph which did, to be fair, parrot back some of the issues I had raised. Sadly, none of these issues were reflected in the body of the proposal, which, like the other two, was clearly a rehash of the bog standard solution. This left me with the incumbent – the fools I wanted to replace in the first place – and so I had to do the pitch all over again. Have you any idea how insulting it can be to your audience to assume that they are exactly the same as any other organisation? Even if you believe they are the same, I can guarantee you that your audience will disagree. Humour them.

> a degree of personalisation is always going to be appropriate

All companies assume themselves to be unique. Therefore, no company is automatically going to assume that a 'standard' offering is going to be right for them. A degree of personalisation is always going to be appropriate, even if it's only a few small changes. These few small changes will make a bigger impact than you might imagine, because they show that you have listened to and taken account of the needs and concerns of your prospect. Your prospect will be pleased. Perhaps they mentioned that support is required only between 8.30 am and 6 pm, in which case don't give them the 'standard' 24-hour service. Supply it only when it's needed, or if you can't supply anything other than 24-hour support knock some money off so the client doesn't have to pay extra for an overspecified service. If you know that your prospect is not a detail person, then don't give them 34 pages of fine detail without a summary section on page 1 – and make sure you have invested time in making the summary both as comprehensive as possible and as short as possible. Equally, if you discover your prospect is cautious and doesn't like leaping into things, suggest a way in which they can buy in smaller stages over a longer period. (By getting them to buy into something smaller now, you will reap the benefits down the line when you have cemented your relationship with them and won their trust.) Small changes with a big impact – why would you not do that, in any pitch scenario?

# CHAPTER 5

# Now do your homework (sorry – no substitute)

Preparation. Why the more you prepare, the luckier you will get. How to structure this phase of the pitch.

When José 'The Special One' Mourinho arrived as manager at Chelsea Football Club, he brought with him a reputation for pre-match planning of the highest order. Each game would be rigorously researched, with detailed briefings on each opposing player, team tactics, diagrams – the works. And it worked. In the book *Leadership – The Lessons of Mourinho*, his wife Tami explains how they generally go out to dinner after each match. 'At the start of the dinner he starts by asking me all about my day and how the children have been. By the middle of dinner he is talking about football, and by dessert he has picked up a piece of paper and starts jotting down notes about the team.' He's barely finished one game and he's already planning for the next. It's a revealing insight, and if we needed a model for how to approach the planning of a pitch we don't need to look much further than Mourinho.

## Corporate autobiography – the annual report

The wider context in which your pitch is taking place is that of the target organisation itself. It may seem difficult to see the relevance of this in some pitch situations, and it's true that if you're pitching something trivial to somebody not very senior it may be completely irrelevant. The more important your pitch is to the target organisation, the more important to your success a deep understanding of that business becomes. Every year businesses set out their stall in writing, in the annual report. Amongst the raw figures you can find the organisation's own interpretation of what it is doing and the reasons why. Sometimes, relevant information can be even easier to spot. In my office there are nearly a hundred annual reports. Most of them contain worthy statements about environmental responsibility, 'green' policies and carbon footprints. But only one of them is bound in recycled cardboard. And so within the first few seconds of picking up their annual report, I've discovered something hugely relevant to anyone pitching to Robert Wiseman Dairies. Who says you can't judge a book by its cover? In a pitch, I would already be thinking about going the extra mile, maybe factoring in some carbon off-setting or something similar to guarantee the greenest solution, in the expectation that the environmental impact could be a deciding factor for this company. And I haven't even read anything inside the report yet.

The chairman's statement will set the scene, and then I usually turn to the pages where they give you information about the board of directors. These may or may not be people you will be pitching to. It is quite possible, however, that they will be cheque-signers or key influencers in the decision. As the most senior staff in the organisation, what they think about things will set the tone for what everybody else thinks about things. If you're pitching at a middle level audience, you should be focusing on the people they report into. Find out how they view the business and the world. Non-executive directors are also of interest, as sometimes the reason for their appointment may shed further light on corporate objectives. It's not unusual for NEDs to be brought in to address a particular issue, and this will probably be in the public domain to impress investors – supply chain management, marketing, export growth, franchising issues. If one of these is on your patch you should be aware of it.

## Corporate unauthorised biography – what the analysts say

If you really want to understand the big picture, you need to ask the analysts. City analysts are a great source of insight. A story in the *Financial* *Times* led to a great opportunity for one of my clients, promoted by something an analyst had noticed. The story appeared in the 'Mudlark' section of the *FT*, which is where the 'funny' stories go (not that they're exactly side-splitting). The analyst had noticed that a UK high street bank had planned to open 70,000 student accounts, but had only achieved around 30,000. The incentive had been a free MP3 player, and the analyst had suggested there must be a warehouse somewhere with the best part of 40,000 MP3 players gathering dust. Cue laughter. Underlying the humorous tone, here was a bank that clearly had a real problem with marketing to students, which in turn was a real opportunity for someone to help them fix it.

> City analysts are a great source of insight

### brilliant tip

Even a relatively brief opinion on a target company provided by an analyst will nevertheless be based on a huge amount of research. Let them do the legwork and the analysis, and you can focus on putting it into action.

You should consider subscribing to analyst information, usually available on a sector basis. And if you pitch to FTSE 250 companies often, you should consider striking up a relationship with a real live analyst. Lunch is a good start.

## Corporate gossip columnists – the trade press

Lunch is also the weapon of choice when it comes to your next source of information – journalists. The trade press knows stuff. Stuff that can be useful. There is almost no corner of industry, commerce and the professions, no matter how tedious, obscure or unloved, which is not served by its own industry rag. If you're selling into a sector you are not totally familiar with, you need to invest in buying a few issues of the key titles. These will quickly give you a flavour of what's happening and what the hot topics are within the sector. They will also allow you to communicate with your prospect using the same language. Jargon excludes people who don't understand; the flip side is that when you are talking the same language, jargon includes you. If you want to talk to major multiple grocers, for example, you would need to know what a SKU is. (It's a stock keeping unit, the little building blocks of retailing.) Little details like this are terribly reassuring to your prospects, whether on a conscious or subconscious level. They signal that you are already part of the same tribe, not an outsider trying to get in. The downside is that you, or someone on your team, will have to spend a lot of hours reading – the sort of reading normally prescribed for insomnia. Instead, spend one hour reading the back issues, and use it to shortlist your journalists – which brings us back to lunch.

Lunch is a far more pleasant alternative to death by trade press. It involves a journalist, who could be a staff or freelance person, simply summarising the issues of the day for you, as well as the latest news from the rumour mill. The journalist lunch is a thoroughly modern, 'interactive' communication method. You can ask questions. You might even share some of your thoughts and your general approach to the pitch, and use them as a sounding board. When short-listing a journalist, I normally start by searching for references to anyone I'm pitching to, plus their superiors in the company. Usually, one or more of them will have been interviewed within the last year, and top of the shortlist should be whoever conducted the interview.

> ### brilliant tip
>
> When you're researching people, you need to find out not just what they do, but also how they do it and what they are like to deal with.

A friend who runs an extremely good brand experience agency told me about a meeting he had, which he described as 'the perfect new business opportunity'. During the course of his meeting with the key decision maker (let's call her Glenda), he had probed a particular topic that a journalist had tipped him off about – Glenda's personal ambitions. A couple of questions about career prospects at the company and the old 'So what's next for you then?' did the trick. Glenda didn't need much encouragement to share her desire to achieve the next level of promotion in the shortest possible time frame. This information was vital. The company for which she worked was by reputation famously cautious. Normally my friend would have couched his pitch in such a way as to play to this corporate character trait. But now he had a new agenda, which was all about 'making Glenda famous'. Now he had a pitch that needed to work on two levels – first, the really ballsy, go-getting pitch to get Glenda on board, and then (in cahoots with Glenda), the more conservative version that would get the project rubber-stamped at a higher level.

All thanks to a journalist.

One last thing: don't forget to exercise a little subtlety in the invitation, perhaps along the following lines. You are about to enter the market, are in the research phase and are just looking for someone friendly to talk to who can give an overview of the

lunch and flattery are
a powerful
combination

marketplace – and your chosen journo has been specially recommended as someone who particularly has their finger on the pulse. Lunch and flattery are a powerful combination.

## What is happening to your target? The competitive perspective

No business exists in isolation. Having a grasp of what your target company's competitors are up to matters, because your target company will have spent more time than you in assessing its own competitive situation. This will have a constant and direct impact on its strategy, if only because the analyst and investor community are constantly benchmarking competitors against one another.

As the CEOs and CFOs do their rounds presenting to City analysts, attempting to talk up the share price, they also have to field questions about competitors. For this, they need answers. Therefore, much of what the company does will necessarily be seen in the context of its competition. It will help you to understand what this context is. Whatever it is you are pitching, from hand dryers to management consultancy services, you need to know what the benefits are *in context*. Will your pitch enable the company to catch up with a competitor? Will it give them a competitive advantage? If the answer to either of these questions is yes, it would be careless of you not to pose these specific questions in the first place. Any good lawyer will tell you that you should never ask a question to which you do not *already* know the answer.

## Corporate culture – how do they buy?

Now that we know about the company, its competitors and the whims and fancies of its senior team, and have taken counsel from people who earn a living from their knowledge of your target company, we need to do some homework on *how they buy*. If you Google the name of your target company alongside words like 'case study', the chances are you will find several examples of work completed on behalf of your prospect. These case studies might be anything from an installation of floor tiles in the staff canteen to a piece of strategic consultancy. You don't know until you look. I can assure you I have found these extremely enlightening on more than one occasion.

Someone's marketing consultancy case study gave one of their competitors a vital steer, enabling them to secure a consulting project from the same buyer. If what you unearth is at all relevant to your own pitch, you can then phone whoever was involved and quiz them about how it came about, how it was sold in, how the buying process worked. Non-competitive suppliers can tell you a great deal. Is your target organisation heavily procurement driven? Do line managers have a lot of autonomy? Ask.

## Who are you up against? Plan to defeat them

In parallel with researching your target, you also need to research your own competition. You need to know what their weaknesses are so you can emphasise features in your own pitch that your competitor will struggle to match. You also need to understand their strengths. If it's a strength you can match, you can eliminate it as a threat. If it's a strength you cannot match then you have a choice to make. If, from your (now excellent) knowledge of the prospect organisation, you feel that it will be seen as 'decision-critical' then one option is to try to close the gap to the point where your other strengths can swing the decision. If this isn't going to be possible, you will have to change the agenda in your favour, by arguing that there is a better alternative. The best way to do this is to take the bull by the horns and tackle the issue head on. If you feel you have a

if you feel you have a weakness, attack is often the best form of defence

weakness, attack is often the best form of defence. You will be in no way apologetic; acknowledge up front the prospect's likely preconception and deal with it. You could start with the 'what you want and what you need are two different things' approach (see Chapter 10 for more on this). The argument typically runs along the following lines:

- My guess is you are looking for X.
- I could have made life easy for myself and come here today loaded up with X.
- But I haven't.
- That's because the best solution for you is actually Y, and here's why . . .

When your opponents are pitching to your prospect, it's likely that they will point to previous examples of how their own particular brand of snake oil has worked wonders. These will probably be exaggerated, or at the very least the evidence will have been manipulated to show things in the best possible light. If you have come up against the competitor before, you may know what their favourite stories are already. If not, you may find them in their own sales collateral. These are probably available online, but it's also worth a call to ask them whether they can mail you some credentials. The stuff they post might be more detailed. When you know what their best stories are you can then research them to see if they can be devalued.

## brilliant tip

Even the strongest competitor will have an Achilles' heel somewhere. You just have to find out what it is and then make sure it becomes a pitch issue.

## Researching your competition

In politics, which seems to me to be a large-scale, ongoing pitch situation, the research function tends to be split into two. There are the people who dig up damaging stories about the opposition, and then there are the people who *make up* damaging stories about the opposition. I shall assume you have higher moral standards than a politician (not hard, is it?) and stick to digging up genuine flaws in your opponent's argument. An obvious starting point is to telephone the clients featured in the case studies. Worst-case scenario is that it really was a fantastic, unmitigated success story. However, the truth is always more complicated. There's always a snag. They may maintain overall that it was a very positive experience, even if it wasn't, as no one likes to admit to making a poor decision, but you can ask different questions to get the desired outcome. It's sometimes best to pose as a potential customer, doing some background checks on a supplier.

The key research questions are leading questions such as, 'Was the outcome exactly what you expected it to be?' (We're looking for a no here – we simply need to be able to say the results achieved did not match the client's expectations.) Always ask whether they plan to repeat the exercise (unless we are talking about something that is clearly a one-off or known to be an infrequent occurrence). There are many reasons, most

> the key research questions are leading questions

of them innocent and unrelated to success or failure, why something may not be repeated. We simply need to be able to say that the client has no plans to repeat it. Ask them outright what things went wrong, however small. A few conversations like this will soon start to build a useful dossier of quotable quotes.

The research phase helps to build the framework upon which you will hang your arguments. In particular, it will flesh out the character of two of the three actors in the drama – your prospect and your competition (the third one being you). It's important to keep this triangular relationship in your mind, because this is how you work out what parts of your research are valuable and what can be discarded. Anything you discover about a competitor will have its meaning defined by how it relates to you and to your prospect. Anything you discover about your prospect will have its meaning defined by how it relates to you and your competitors. Along with the more challenging parts of the research effort, there will of course be more mundane fact-gathering to be done. There is no secret about how to do this beyond, I suppose, simply making sure that someone does actually do it.

The thing about research is that you often don't realise the significance of information until the right context presents itself. I learned something about that from, of all things, an episode of *Antiques Roadshow*. One of the experts had made a particular study of a small school of artists, and over the years had come to know a phenomenal amount about them – the tell-tale brush strokes, the choice of subject, the colour palette. He had spotted a painting in a sale that he thought might possibly belong to the same school, although it hadn't been attributed as such. He bought it for not very much money, and his hunch proved correct. It is now worth the sort of money that buys a very large house.

'Fortune,' he said, 'favours the prepared.'

# CHAPTER 6

# The most important 'p' in pitch ... is people

It's all about you, and it's all about them. The importance of people and personalities in getting your pitch just right.

You might imagine that a pitch by an advertising agency, to a major brand-owning organisation, based on a clear brief, using a lengthy and thorough process and involving detailed stages of strategic analysis, research and creativity, would end up with a decision that was both evidence-based and objective.

Go on, you would, wouldn't you?

Again, sorry to disappoint you. I have personally seen (as have lots of the people I know) many situations where the client has seemingly made the 'wrong' choice, based on any objective, independent review of the evidence. Why? Well, I know the answer to this because I've done it myself. Having reviewed the evidence carefully, and reached a conclusion about the pros and cons of the various bids in front of me, I have then consciously ignored it and made my decision on the basis of the *people*. And it's been the right decision.

## When you are pitching, *you* are a big part of what you are selling

Choosing a plumber was what opened my eyes. I had this plumber who was very good, and reasonably priced, but every single time he came round I would get a very, very long lecture on the history and structure of my plumbing, the shortcomings of my boiler and an outline of the many options that now lay before me. What I actually wanted was a clear recommendation, and that was the one thing I never got. I simply wanted to know what, in his expert opinion, I should actually do! How hard is that? So when the time came to replace the boiler I got a couple of quotes. My plumber was as cheap as anyone else, knew my existing system inside out already and could do the job earlier than anyone else. I chose the more expensive quote, and chose to wait longer for the job to be done, for the simple reason that I couldn't bear the thought of having to listen to my plumber's inconclusive blithering any more. I chose the person despite the apparent merits of the pitch.

Martin Jones, who ran an organisation called the Advertising Agency Register (a kind of 'marriage broker' between clients and agencies), once gave me a great piece of advice. At the end of the day, pitch decisions often boil down to the fact that 'people buy people'. It's stuck in my mind because over the years that view has been validated over and over again, from my own choice of plumber to some of the most valuable advertising contracts in the entire country. So what do you do with that information? Can you make yourself 'likeable'? At the very least, and I mean the very least, you *can* avoid the things that tend to count against businesspeople and plumbers. Even better, you can adopt some simple behaviours that will help your target audience warm to you on a personal level.

> pitch decisions often boil down to the fact that 'people buy people'

## brilliant tip

The most important ingredient in any pitch is personal chemistry – the way the people on both sides of the fence interact with each other. Getting this right is the single most important factor influencing success.

## Shut up and have a conversation

Think back to the occasions when you've really enjoyed a conversation with somebody and got on with them really well. I would suggest to you that on many of the occasions when you think you've had a great *conversation* – implying a mutual exchange – it has in reality been pretty one-sided, and you did most of the talking yourself. For most people, a really good conversation is one centred around themselves.

Think about the times when someone you know well has reported back to you that they've had a great time in someone's company. You may have observed this phenomenon. I had a client once who had come along with her boss, me and my colleague for an after-work drink. I'd chatted to her boss and she'd been talking to my colleague. The next day she mentioned on the phone how much she'd enjoyed the evening and what a really great conversation she'd had. And yet I'd noticed that for the entire duration of the 'conversation' she had been the one doing the talking. My unfortunate colleague would nod, raise and lower eyebrows as appropriate and occasionally chuck in a 'continuity' question like, 'No! So what happened then?' Quite a difference between perception and reality.

## Why do you like the people you like?

What sort of people do you like? They probably share some characteristics. They probably show some interest in you. They probably ask a lot of questions and avoid talking about themselves the whole time. They probably put you at ease when you are in their company. They're probably easy to talk to (which usually means they are good listeners). They are interesting and interested. There's no rocket science there, but you would be amazed how often these basic rules are ignored. It also helps if you have something in common. In a pitch situation, you should assume that you *do* have something in common with the people you're pitching to, which means your problem is simply to establish what it is. You should do this well in advance.

I've had clients over the years who have had particularly unusual interests. One was an enthusiastic amateur military historian and used to spend weekends dressed up in seventeenth century gear, re-enacting battles from the English Civil War. Another had a large collection of blue note jazz vinyl. One of them even kept snakes: in the evening she would kill small rodents by putting them in a cloth bag and hitting the bag against a wall, to turn them into snake food. Even an obscure interest can be an opening for you. You can quickly become knowledgeable on just about any subject thanks to the internet – knowledgeable enough to establish a rapport with your target prospect, who will be thrilled to have discovered a fellow morris dancing enthusiast. So go ahead, invent a shared interest; make it up and make yourself interesting.

Mainly, the connections and shared interests are of the more 'normal' variety. A colleague of mine happened to be making small talk of the 'what have you got planned for the weekend?' variety, when it became apparent that she and the prospect were both outdoorsy hillwalking types. They then started comparing notes on 'approach shoes' and they were away. New best friends. If you can make this kind of connection in the early stages of the pitch process, you are in a highly advantageous position. I still don't know what an 'approach shoe' is.

## The importance of trust

Another question to ask yourself is this: what sort of people do I like *professionally*? What would you look for if you were buying services in a business context, and you're the customer not the salesperson? They're probably all the things we looked at above, plus some other important factors. They would probably give you a sense of confidence (a safe pair of hands); you'd be looking for reassurance that they would act in your best interests, give you good advice, be honest with you, be reliable.

I wonder if you remember the 'quality' fad from some years back? In the UK it started with something called BS 5750, and before we knew it it had turned into ISO 9000. Who knows what it is nowadays. It spawned a generation of quality 'consultants', professional nit-pickers like the one who turned up at a friend's digital marketing agency and wanted to know where the 'non-conforming product area' was. (The 'recycle bin' on the computer in this instance.) The one thing that the quality fad had to offer to those of us who *didn't* work in factories making widgets was this simple idea: 'Say what you do; do what you say.' This simple sentence, when put into practice, is the thing that makes you reliable. No one wants to work with people who are unreliable. A lot of desirable features can be summed up by the word trust. Trust is the bedrock of a good business relationship.

> trust is the bedrock of a good business relationship

## Building belief

How do you establish trust with someone you don't know? There are a number of ways to do this. Trust is simply belief, and belief is a lot easier to create when you have some hard evidence. Endorsements from current and previous clients are a good start. Endorsements that confirm that you say what you do and do what you say, and perhaps also do it fast, cheap, to a high standard or whatever attributes best suit your pitch. If you have these to hand, make sure you use them. If not, get some. Even better, write the endorsements yourself and ask your favourite clients to sign them. Public relations is another route, but *not* one that is going to work within a pitch timescale. You should be considering raising your profile in a positive way through PR so that when the time comes to pitch, you can point to positive stories in the trade press.

 **tip**

> Real trust has to be earned. The *expectation* of trustworthiness can be established in the mind of a prospect in advance of actually earning it.

Then there are awards. There are plenty of these to choose from, and with a little application you should be able to collect one or two that sound reasonably impressive and can be wheeled out at pitch time. In the world of creative agencies, awards for creativity are highly prized – from Golden Lions to Yellow Pencils to Best anything you like. However, if you ask the opinion of the people who pay for the work – the clients – you will usually hear that creative awards are all well and good, but the awards they pay most attention to, and are most convincing in a pitch environment, are those concerning *effectiveness*. Awards that demonstrate more commercial benefits such as return on investment, increase in sales or market share – evidence that the creative work *worked*. Enter an awards' competition so long as the resulting prize is going to work hard for you as an asset in business development.

## Finding the people behind the job title

So, in order to engage with your decision makers as people, and thus bond with them and create trust, your early priority has to be to find out as much as you can about them. Not merely on a professional level, but also on a personal level. There are many ways of doing this. An obvious source is the internet. Potentially, you might find out something interesting from the social networks. However, in my experience it's not often you find anything interesting about the more senior prospects on the likes of Facebook. The junior prospects may well be out there, and if you find something you should go ahead and use it. So what are we looking for?

First, their origins. Where do they come from? Where did they go to school? Where did they go to university? Maybe there is a connection to be made through geography and educational history. When they were at university, what did they do? Perhaps they supply news about themselves to an alumni network? More importantly, what do they do *now*? Sports and hobbies are highly relevant, but keep an open mind as you never know what you might turn up. If the internet fails to deliver (unlikely, if you try hard enough and use some ingenuity and lateral thinking) then you could try talking to a real person. In the past I've found out about people through all kinds of means. Phoning up to ask advice about 'buying a present' is an unusual example but has been known to work. Colleagues will often tell you stuff about people they work with, if you ask. Think of it as being one of the fun parts of the pitch process.

An IT sales professional told me that his first major sale was to a delightful old gentleman who worked in a 'deep staff' department of a bank. A couple of weeks after winning the pitch, when the pressure was off, he asked him the reason for his decision. More persuasive benefits? Better reference sites? Cheaper solution? None of these, in fact. The reason was that this particular solution would allow him to leave earlier, and thus in the summer give him more time to tend the love of his life – his rose garden. With hindsight (a wonderful thing), it may have been possible to establish that particular personal requirement *before* the pitch, but only *if* you had already decided to make people a priority.

The more senior your targets, the easier it gets to find out about them. The investor sections of corporate websites frequently contain short biographies of the directors. If the person has ever spoken at a conference, there will be information about them available online. Really senior targets (such as major corporation chairmen and their 'C-suite' colleagues) may appear in directories like *Who's Who*. A company I was working for once needed to get through to the CEO of a large organisation to influence the outcome of a pitch. It wasn't working, and his PA (a hybrid creature somewhere between a hyena and a pit bull terrier) wouldn't let us anywhere near. Finally, I was able to get a message through to him when we found out he was a member of a London club. A hand-written note, personally delivered to the club, was eventually picked up a week later, and I like to think the CEO's decision to get back in touch with us was made over a Scotch and soda at the club, whilst seated in his favourite leather armchair.

## Knowledge is power – use it to build a relationship

Having found your information, use some common sense in applying it. I happen to be a player of the Great Highland Bagpipe. It wouldn't take me long to work out what level of knowledge you had of the pipes once we started talking about it. But you could claim a peripheral interest and then say something sensible on the subject. Or we could just talk about the shared experience of learning to play a musical instrument. Those conversations would stick in my mind a lot longer than the conversations we might have about purely work-related matters.

Some people may think it's difficult, false and slightly absurd to turn the conversation around during a pitch to feeding small rodents to pet snakes. This is indeed true, but consider the following point. If the first time you really get to talk to your prospects is in the final set-piece pitch, you've probably already lost. Or more to the point, someone else has already won. Material of this kind should be deployed from the very early stages of the pitch process (it's always a process of some kind). It has a second role, too. Through a better understanding of the character and personalities of the people to whom you are going to pitch, you might conclude that you need to change the people on your own team. These little personal details can give you crucial insights into the human issues of the pitch.

## Use your knowledge of the prospect's team to shape your own

Casting is important, because personal chemistry is important. I've mentioned already the business-to-business 'speed dating' events that we run. Each session lasts 11 minutes. It's very successful and is a logical consequence of the 'people buy people' theory – personal chemistry is an important part of the

> casting is important, because personal chemistry is important

buying process, but that can be established within minutes. As a seller, it's every bit as useful to know that the buyer thinks their people could never work with your people as to discover that you get on like a house on fire. It saves a lot of wasted time, for both parties. A key benefit of researching the individuals on the buying team is that you can maximise your chances of positive personal chemistry – simply by fielding the right sort of people. If you can compose your team so that it contains not only the right skills, but also the right mix of personalities, you will straight away be one step ahead of a competitor that has a similar product or skill set to you, but is *not* going to hit it off on a personal level with the buyers. In fact, picking the right pitch team is probably the simplest yet most important thing you can do. Did I say the simplest? I lied.

Individual team members will always have gaps in their skills and capabilities. You need to ensure the team as a whole has every angle covered. This is about finding the right mix of complementary strengths.

There are three qualities to consider in selecting someone for a pitch team:

1  What are they like, as people?

2  What do they know, as professionals?

3  How do they come across in a pitch situation?

The latter element can be worked on, through training, personal development and so on. However, this takes time, so you need to be sure that whoever you pick at this stage is already up to scratch, or nearly so. You will find it almost impossible to identify individuals who tick all three boxes. A person who has the right mix of professional skills, can handle themselves well in a pitch *and* just happens to be perfect casting for your buyers is rare, and you can count yourself lucky when you find one! Mostly it will be a case of two out of three ain't bad. However, across the pitch team as a whole you not only can, but *must* tick each of the three boxes. Your team must contain the knowledge and experience to field the most difficult questions, the right personal qualities to bond with the buyers at a personal level and the skills required to manipulate the course of the pitch. And as with any team, each member needs to be clear about exactly what their role is, and what they are meant to be doing, when, and why. In the next chapter we'll take a look at that.

# CHAPTER 7

# About teamwork

Some simple ways of choosing a recipe that makes the most of your raw ingredients.

I t may seem obvious, but when you are pitching as a team, the team members need to have a shared understanding of what is (and isn't) going to happen during the pitch. Take the following example. A team from a large multinational advertising agency is pitching to a major banking group. The 'creative' section of the pitch, in which the agency talks about the end product, has just begun. The presenter is a senior creative person. Having explained the idea and talked through the script for the TV commercial, he then tells them that he has the perfect soundtrack. He had heard it that very morning and was blown away by how perfect it would be.

A fly on the wall in the pitch would now be noticing the other members of the agency team squirming in their seats ever so slightly. This (literally) wasn't in the script. But it's already too late. The hovering finger now presses the Play button, soon filling the room with the strains of 'Especially for You' by Jason and Kylie. If the senior creative had chosen his tune well, there might have been some benefit in the prospect seeing those agency faces light up in a spontaneous display of delight. As it was, all the prospect got to see was the fleeting exchange of horrified glances; momentary, but as plain to see as if they'd been flashed around the room by a signal lamp from a battleship. One of the agency people in the room at the time later told me, 'I was so embarrassed I just sat there seething. I may have poisoned the atmosphere. I don't care. If we'd made that commercial I'd never have been able to live it down.'

No surprises. You need to insist on that, or your pitch could backfire on you. The agency in the example above failed to win the pitch, and that's no surprise either. Teamwork is about avoiding surprises.

## Process – why little and often beats long and occasional

Rehearsal is a key part of that process and should start very early on. The 'shape' of the pitch content should be grounded as soon as possible. That way, you can refine the content into seamless modules that fit together, in the right order. Having started by establishing a 'helicopter' view of the pitch structure, you can then refine down the content as you go forward. The temptation is then to let the individual team members go off and generate the content for their own section. This is where things can unravel. It's surprising how 'out of shape' a pitch can get if left unattended for long enough. The team leader needs to legislate a process by which the content is regularly reviewed, not just in its sectional silos, but also within the overall context. The way to do this is to structure your process on the 'little and often' principle. Meet regularly, and make it short whenever you can. Big, long set-piece meetings are frustrating for all concerned. What tends to happen is that as an issue arises, much time will be devoted to resolving it. You will then have the other team members not associated with this particular issue getting increasingly frustrated about being in the room. They could be elsewhere, doing something useful instead.

### brilliant tip

Scheduling pitch development meetings isn't just about diary management, it's also about keeping your team members mentally fresh and engaged through the process.

There are many books you can buy on the subject of teamwork, and many companies spend large amounts of money on training and consultancy to help their people work better as a team. But a pitch is different. It has an objective and a scope, and will be undertaken in a finite period of time. Most times, you will have little flexibility in the personnel available to you. And also, most of the time, decisions about the structure of the pitch will be made for the wrong reasons.

## It's always start-again time (beware of habitual behaviour)

Advertising agencies are a great example of this. Because they comprise various departments which work together on *existing* clients, that structure becomes, by default, the preferred structure for pitching. So the planner will do the planning part, the creative director will probably present the work, the media person will do the media bit and the senior management will top and tail the pitch. Decisions will also be made on the basis of who is deemed to be 'good at presenting' and what things the prospect ought to be most interested in. In advertising the 'product' is the creative work. Therefore, much time is spent setting up the underlying rationale (this is the bit the planner will probably do)

> in advertising the 'product' is the creative work

and then much time will also be spent on showing off the work to its best advantage. The final bit will be the media section, as this is considered to be like plumbing – necessary, but not particularly interesting and something that is not inherently 'creative'. It all seems logical to a point, but it simply mirrors their own preconceptions, not the desires of the people they may be pitching to.

Simon Marquis, an advertising industry consultant, used to be an agency media person. He tells of a pitch in which, true to form, the media section had been relegated to the last part of the afternoon's proceedings. It was an important pitch, and he had sweated for many hours over the media planning, the costings, the audience delivery, the day-part analysis of the proposed TV media schedule, the audience demographics and much more besides. Five weeks of hard work had gone into this. On the day of the pitch, the strategy section and the creative section had both overrun by quite a margin, leaving about 14 seconds in which to cover the media strategy. At this point, the senior agency person made his apologies for running out of time to cover the media section, offering to 'send that bit on to you in the post'. Simon was not the only one infuriated by this. The client revealed that it was, in fact, the media section in which he was most interested. What effort would have been required to discover that in advance? Not much, I suspect. A common pitfall in pitching is that it is all too easy for your existing world view to drive a process that must instead be driven by the needs of your prospect. In this instance, the teamwork failed because the structure was wrong, the assumptions were wrong and the people in the pitch couldn't keep to their timing schedule – or, worse, just couldn't be bothered to.

In a prospect-centric view of pitching (which is the premise of this argument) that would never have happened. The team would have been constructed in line with the requirements of the audience, with the appropriate amount of time and attention allocated accordingly.

## The right people for a pitch team aren't always the obvious people

In a completely different sector, software, a company was invited to present to a director of a major supermarket on how they might help to improve sales through the use of the customer database. They had a pitch team of five, including the database guru in case things got really technical. Database gurus being what they are, the company didn't usually bring him out in front of real prospects; but they only had this one chance to impress, and the pitch leader didn't want to leave without having answered any question that might be thrown at him. The pitch leader duly instructed the guru to sit in silence unless specifically spoken to, and then to restrict himself to single sentence answers. At the start of the pitch the team was introduced. The director of the supermarket said that his company's experience was that the best solutions were those where there was a good match between the technology and the business need. He then rounded on the technical guru and asked him to spend some time describing what he felt to be the supermarket's business need and, in the light of that, the relevance to them of the technology being proposed. More for form's sake than anything else, the pitch leader had (thankfully) included him in the internal pre-pitch discussions and meetings. To the amazement of the other four members of the pitch team, the database guru promptly spoke for 20 minutes without any slides or props and did a superb job. They won the business – but only on the basis that the guru was assigned permanently to the project.

Hats off to the director of the supermarket, I think, for asking an intelligent and incisive question – and putting it to the right person. Half the battle in getting pitch teams to work effectively is having the right people on the team in the first place, and anticipating accurately what their role really needs to be. That role needs to be what your prospect needs it to be, whether you're selling an advertising campaign or a database software solution. This can be sometimes hard to discern from within your own organisation because of the mental baggage we all carry around with us. Objectivity is called for. I would recommend to you that you take on board an external resource to act as 'pitch doctor'.

## Time to doctor your pitch

The role of the pitch doctor is an important one. From the very start, they can provide that objectivity which is so hard to achieve from an internal source. A pitch doctor can cut across the normal internal barriers. These can be barriers that exist through departmental demarcation lines or barriers of hierarchy, prejudice and preconception. They can help you to ensure that your intelligence gathering activity – vital, as we have seen, in the early phases – is turned into actionable output that reflects accurately what has been learned. Too often, it is simply force-fitted into an existing internal shape. They may also have a broader contextual view that will be of value – perhaps experience from across different industries and sectors – and they should be a source of the latest knowledge and thinking around the matter in hand.

 **brilliant** tip

In Shakespeare's *King Lear*, the Fool is perhaps the only character able both to discern the truth of the situation and to tell the King what he really thinks. Every pitch leader needs a good fool.

Pitch Doctor is a role I've performed many times, and in every case an early issue is to do with the team structure. I point out that there is a series of logical steps that needs to take place, at the end of which we can address the specifics of how the team work together as individuals. Many of these logical steps are covered in the early part of this book – being clear about what the prospect is really looking for, doing the homework, getting close to the prospect on a personal level. These findings will shape your team, at a functional level, and the individuals will then fall into place – but now on the basis of the requirements of the prospect. The individuals themselves may be a case of 'it is what it is' – you may be stuck with them and have to make the best of it. Teamwork is not a black art, it's very obvious. The answer to how best to run the team will always lie inside your own head, not inside mine. You will know what they are like as individuals – loud, aggressive, lazy, charismatic, silent. Brian Clough, the football manager, achieved great success not because of but perhaps *in spite* of the quality of his individual players. He understood what they were capable of, moulded them into the right shape and then inspired them to go the extra mile, individually and collectively. It was a team effort.

## Interrogate your colleagues

To find out what your people are capable of, you need to ask them. A teamwork exercise conducted at Harvard was based around an ambitious project – going to the

> to find out what your people are capable of, you need to ask them

moon. The various students were put into teams and had to work together to work out how to achieve the objective. After much effort the various teams came back together and the presentations and findings were debriefed. One key finding revolved around the fact that one of the groups had been seeded with a particular individual. He hadn't said very much at all, in fact he had contributed very little to his group's output. This had been noticed in passing, but the ambitious young things at Harvard hadn't bothered themselves too much about it as they were all in the business of making themselves look as fabulous as possible. The person in question was in fact an astronaut.

Having established whether you may have any astronauts, you will discover that you haven't – it's a radical example to prove a point. But you will discover that there is *more* relevant know-how among your team members than you may have given them credit for. Then you have to put it to work.

Your early phase of research will have determined the key areas that you need to cover, what the priority concerns of the client are, and you will have formulated a structure to your pitch accordingly. It should now be clear to you how the roles and responsibilities of the team should be demarcated.

## Who, how many and why?

A common question is, 'How many people should we take?' This is usually an issue of seniority rather than quantity of attendees. Should it be senior people or the whole team, or what? Some clients like to meet the entire team working on their business while others prefer just to deal with the top people in the company. Usually I would advise that you start 'big' and tell your prospect that you are prepared to bring along everyone to the pitch, as some clients like to be able to see exactly who is involved. The suggestion in itself communicates a high level of commitment. You can then establish whether or not they are that sort of client. If they don't feel it's necessary to meet everyone they are unlikely to go along with you turning up with a cast of thousands.

One big decision will be, 'Who's going to present what?' I have never been a fan of having a big team in which everyone presents a little bit – usually done because someone has decided that everyone should have a role. Delivering the pitch is not everyone's role. There is a child's game in which little heads pop up randomly for a short time, and the game is to bash them with a hammer before they disappear again. To people on the receiving end of pitches, the desire to bash down the endless procession of pop-up presenters can be an all too familiar emotion. Having lots of heads pop up and go away again disrupts the flow of the pitch. If there is a narrative to what you are putting forward – and there should be – then you need to deliver the pitch in a way that does not artificially disrupt the flow. This will mean having a small number of people whose job it is to present, and maybe some

> delivering the pitch is not everyone's role

others who field questions on various aspects. Harking back to the database guru example, your process would in that instance have revealed the client's key concerns much earlier, and he would have been identified as a key presenter well ahead of pitch day. The same would have been true in the Simon Marquis media story.

# CHAPTER 8

# The time to win the pitch is before you do the pitch

How to ensure success by loading the dice in your favour before you even deliver the pitch.

It's the big day – pitch day.

For some, this is the moment of truth, the one defining hour in which everything comes together in the climax that is the pitch itself. For these people, the likely outcome is defeat. Because if you've left it all down to pitch day, and your success is down to how well you perform in the pitch itself, then you have left it too late. Your objective must be this: to have as good as won the pitch before you even open the door to the pitch room.

## The importance of starting off in front

Here is one of the most effective methods. In a process hijack you engage with the prospect *very* early on, in a working environment in which you *jointly* redefine the problem, and thus load the dice in your favour. The more 'consultative' the service you are pitching, the more appropriate this method is, but its applications are surprisingly broad. A marketing director told me about an experience he had had while running a pitch for his advertising business. One of the agencies had insisted on an initial working session to discuss the brief, attended by the key members of the marketing and agency teams. While it was time consuming, he agreed on the basis that if it was going to increase the chances of generating a better result for himself, it was worth playing along. The process ran like this. The agency had identified four key areas for consideration – the product, the audience, the corporate vision and the market potential. The assembled folk were then split into four teams, each a mixture of client and agency people, and each team went away to consider one of the four topics. After due consideration and debate, the results were debriefed and posted on to a wall. Key to the process was the input of the agency's best strategic brains and the way the discussion unfolded as a seemingly joint enterprise. So, by the end of it, not only had the agenda been recast in the image of the day's discussions, but the intellectual and emotional ownership of it now resided with the team – and it was, above all, a shared ownership.

The agency is now in a vastly stronger position than any other competitor. Even if the client feeds the new brief into the other competing agencies, which is entirely possible, the others can never fully grasp the thought process that led to the changes – because they weren't there when it happened. Furthermore, while the other competitors are still viewed as contenders, one contender is already acting like a partner.

## brilliant tip

Engaging your prospect very early on to shape their requirements is not optional. If you don't do it, one of your competitors surely will and your chances of victory are halved.

The crucial difference with this approach is that the agency is not seeking to gain a fuller understanding of the brief. They are instead seeking to evolve the brief itself and to be part of that evolution. You may in the past have spent time with your prospects prior to a pitch. You have probably been engaged in the worthy endeavour of trying to understand every aspect of the client's requirements, to eliminate any trace of misunderstanding. All well and good, but you have to deal with the possibility that in the meantime someone else has been hijacking the process. What you come away with from the standard approach is, at best, a completely accurate grasp of what your prospects thought they wanted yesterday. That's because your early engagement with the prospect is one of discovery. To me this feels like archaeology, like digging up what's already there.

The process I have just described is not archaeology, it's creativity. When you think of it in these terms, you are not going to spend any more time questioning your prospect to gain a better understanding of their brief.

> while doing a pitch is an event, winning a pitch is very much a process

Instead, you are going to seek to work with them to evolve their understanding of their own needs. You're going to work with them to reshape this requirement, and this is one way in which you will start to win the pitch before it happens. While doing a pitch is an event, winning a pitch is very much a *process*.

## Engaging with a reluctant prospect

What if they just point-blank refuse to get drawn into a process hijack? It's a good question, and a common one. If there are a number of contenders in the frame, it's very possible that a buyer will take the view that any time spent with them should be rationed and that the competitors should get equal amounts of time. So if one of them wants to do a half-day workshop the answer will be no, because the buyer isn't going to invest that amount of time in each competitor. Do not despair. There are other things that can be done, which take less time, but still provide the right forum for engaging with your targets.

In the creative and consulting industries this is quite easy to engineer. Creative pitches are by definition going to involve a presentation of creative work. It's quite easy to request one or more interim meetings. One such meeting type is the 'tissue meeting'. Here ideas can be floated and reactions gauged in order to refine direction. The weaker ideas get ripped up (as though they were on tissue paper) and chucked straight in the bin. One or two of the ideas will inevitably gain some traction, and this allows the pitching company to get a better feel for the kind of work this prospect is going to buy. So, at this stage, the role of the work being presented is diagnostic – it's not the real deal yet. It's purpose is to narrow down the available territory prior to further creative development. This is obviously a positive thing for your pitch. Your chances of winning are always going to be better when you know that *all* your ideas are along the right lines to begin with. Your prospects should not object to this kind of request. You should stress that in return for a small investment in time, the content of the pitch is going to be a much tighter fit with the customer's requirements, and that is surely a good thing for any buyer.

It's also very possible to combine your 'research' phase with your 'engagement' activity in order to kill two birds with one stone. 'Visiting' is one way to do this. Your buyer will be instantly impressed by the thoroughness of your research when you get into visitor mode. It may be a factory, a call centre, a distribution depot, a training facility – there's always something out there to visit that will be in some way relevant. An agency I once worked for pitched for the Marie Curie Cancer Care account. I had to spend a day in one of their cancer hospices, a day that was by a very long way the most challenging day at work I have ever spent. I was in the company of one of the people we were eventually going to pitch to, and neither of us was able to guess what the most popular drink in the hospice was. Orange juice? Tea? Actually it's gin and tonic. These are terminal patients, and their average life expectancy at the point of admission is 16 days. It was quite an experience to share. But I think it helped us both to win the pitch and to do a better job on their behalf subsequently.

brilliant tip

'Researching' isn't just about finding things out. It should be a process designed to help you build relationships with the prospect organisation.

These encounters will help you to uncover the real issues. If you don't identify the real issues, situations like the following can occur. A salesperson was pitching to the board of a building society about putting new technology in the hands of branch counter staff. After an hour's presentation covering technology, and a detailed cost-benefit analysis, he asked if there were any questions. The managing director said he had one: 'That's all very interesting but how will it solve one of our major in-branch problems? How will it put a smile on the faces of our cashiers when they talk to customers?' By the time the pitch comes around, it's too late to address issues like this one, which, though it came from left-field, was eminently discoverable in the earlier stages by spending some time in the branch.

Your immediate prospect may or may not attend your onsite visits (they frequently do – especially in large organisations where people tend to lose touch with what's out there in their own organisation), but you can extract value in either case. If your buyer is not there when you visit, and you're shown around by someone else, you should be able to mine the hapless colleague for a large amount of valuable information. They will simply assume that their role is to tell you everything you want to know.

Another tactic is to suggest a series of short but frequent 'checkpoint' meetings. The purpose would be for you to share with the prospect some of your thinking as it develops, to act as a reality check, and also to give you the benefit of some feedback and input from the prospect. Again, this is pitched as a way of max-imising the chances of hitting the bullseye on pitch day in the best interests of the buyer. You have to offer something in return, however, and it is this: not to phone them up the whole time in between meetings. Your prospect may well buy into this. One thing that quickly becomes an irritation is pitch competitors constantly calling up with spurious requests. Why people do this I don't know. Well I do – it's because they've been taught to keep in touch with their prospects to keep them warm. When you're on the receiving end, you quickly come to dread the twice-daily message that, 'Bob from Rainbow Box and Carton called . . . again.' (Meaning, Bob's thought up yet another pointless and trivial excuse to 'keep the relationship warm'.) Good luck with that one Bob, because one good face-to-face is worth any amount of phone calls. There is another reason why these face-to-face meetings are so valuable. They give you a chance to discover one other piece of priceless information. And it's a piece of information almost nobody ever bothers to look for.

## Learning how your prospect's brain processes information

If you talk to educationalists, they will tell you that people learn in different ways. You may have heard that. However, you may not be aware how pronounced the differences can be. An idea expressed in words might be virtually incomprehensible to certain people – and yet when expressed pictorially the very same idea can suddenly make all the sense in the world. It's like turning on the light in a darkened room. Simply by presenting information in the right way, you can improve your chances of success – just as by presenting information in the wrong way, you can damage your chances.

> by presenting information in the right way, you can improve your chances of success

There are various models of 'learning style'. My personal favourite was first put forward by Richard Felder and Linda Silverman over 20 years ago in their 1988 paper, 'Learning and teaching styles in engineering education', (*Engineering Education*, 78(7), 674–681).

They identified four learning dimensions (these are the updated versions) – namely:

- active and reflective;
- sensing and intuitive;
- visual and verbal;
- sequential and global.

In a pitch scenario it is the last two dimensions that are of the most practical use.

Visual learners (and this is the largest of the groups) learn best in the ways you might expect – pictures, charts, diagrams, video, demonstrations and so on.

Verbal learners on the other hand get more out of language, whether written or spoken. For the avoidance of doubt, a PowerPoint presentation with lots of words doesn't count as 'visual' communication. Cognitive scientists suggest that when people see words on a screen, the brain 'reads' them and processes them the same as the spoken word. The process will take time and your audience will lose the thread.

Sequential learners like arguments to be presented in a logical series of bite-sized chunks. Bottom-up, if you like.

With global learners it's more top-down. Global learners prefer the bigger picture first, before drilling down into the details. Global learners can absorb lots of information, but struggle to do anything with it, before they get to the 'Oh right – I get it!' moment. I am, I think, a mainly visual and global sort of learner.

So, if you try to explain something to me (whatever its merits) in a verbal and sequential way, I'm just going to find it harder to take in, and I'll also find the whole process more frustrating. I'll lose my concentration earlier, and I might just lose my patience too. But if you knew that, you'd give me something highly visual, and give me the big picture right up front so I can immediately get everything into context.

### brilliant tip

When you know how your prospect processes information, you can dramatically improve the impact of your pitch by presenting information in the right way.

How do you spot who's who? I said that I was a global sort of learner and, according to my educationalist friend Steve Lee, I'm in good company – most of the male members of the population, in fact. It turns out that gender has a bearing on this, and educationalists have discovered that boys like to be able to see the bigger picture, to know the context within which the information exists – they need to know what 'the point' of something is. Girls, however, are very capable of working in a sequential way and can deal with information in a more abstract manner. The verbal and visual dimension is trickier, and we don't have the benefit of the sweeping generalisation to assist us. But if I try to explain something to you and I notice your eyes rolling upwards, I know that what you're probably doing is trying to convert what I'm telling you into a picture in your own mind. You're visual. If I notice you are listening intently to what I'm saying then I will guess you are verbal. So either way, I now know how I'm going to make it really easy for you to 'get' whatever it is I'm trying to communicate. My competitors might simply frustrate you – and not even realise they're doing it. Wonderful.

## Professional relationships are like personal ones – a two-way street

These early meetings are not just going to establish what you think of the buyer – what they're like, what their agendas really are, how best to communicate with them – they are also going to establish what the buyer thinks of you. It is vitally important in these early stages of the pitch that you and your team are at the top of your game, and then some. If you say you're going to do something, be somewhere or supply something, then you absolutely have to do/be/supply without fail, faultlessly – on time, no excuses. You have to treat these meetings as more important than the pitch itself. Your objective is for the prospect to be thoroughly impressed by your professionalism, by your people – by everything about you. It will be a lasting impression. Here's why: cognitive dissonance.

Cognitive dissonance is a marvellous thing. Get it right and it's like putting your buyer on autopilot, all the way to the signed cheque. It works like this. Holding two contradictory ideas in your head at once is uncomfortable for most people. Once people have formed an opinion about something, they tend to notice the evidence that validates their choice – and tend to ignore the things that contradict it (the things that create dissonance).

This can work for you. Use this early contact to impress them – anything that can communicate positive attributes like speed, quality, intelligence and reliability should be seized upon. If you say you're going to get back to the buyer about something, get back to them

> use this early contact to impress them

*now* and make the response *great*. Gear up your team from day one to treat any communication with the prospect, however trivial, as an absolutely top priority. These early contacts will position all the competitors in any pitch relative to each other. It's far better to start in pole position than have to claw your way back from a negative perception. Like everything, it's one more opportunity to get one over on the competition.

## Everything is an opportunity to impress

Even unwelcome developments such as a tight deadline can be an opportunity to get one over on your competition. We've all been in the situation where the submission has to be in by a particular date – sometimes even a particular time on that date. As is the way of the world, time is probably not on your side. Many people would take the view that for resource planning reasons, the thing to do is work back from the due date and schedule in everyone to do their bit, review and revise according to a tightly managed plan. This should, and indeed usually does, ensure the proposal goes in on time.

Meanwhile, on the buyer's side of the fence, here's what happens: not very much. Until the due date arrives, at which point within the space of a couple of hours various participants deliver their proposals. The buyers now have an in-tray bigger than Gibbon's *The Decline and Fall of the Roman Empire*. And your opportunity to gain a competitive advantage has been missed.

### brilliant tip

In new business, timing is everything. Timing is just as important in the less obvious ways – like the timing of a pitch submission.

Consider this example. A company I work with were given ten working days to pull together a proposal that would determine whether or not they move from the long list to the pitch list. At this point they decided to make sure the proposal was submitted by 8.30 am *the day before* the deadline. It was a struggle, but it was done. Two months later, having not only got on the pitch list but won the job, the client revealed that because the original proposal had arrived early, the buying team had actually spent an hour and a half going through it. Its contents had stimulated discussion among the buying team about the options and priorities and key decision-making criteria. This had in turn helped to shape the eventual pitch. The following day – deadline day – all the other entries came in and each one was given less than half the time devoted to the early bird.

I recall a pitch from a few years back where the company we were pitching to, which had been under some pressure, ran into further difficulties – which in turn caused a postponement of the pitch. They phoned all the competitors offering new dates for a couple of months hence and asked us to pick a slot to come in to pitch. The response from us was a call back with a strong argument in favour of not delaying the pitch, but bringing it forward instead. We explained we had a clear point of view about this and were in a position to come in and pitch right now. We argued that doing nothing was no longer a realistic option, and our ideas would help them embark upon a fresh, positive course of action.

The tactic of challenging the basic assumptions around a pitch scenario can be a high-risk strategy, but in the instance above it clearly positioned our company as one with a positive and proactive attitude. Our view was that whether they accepted the proposal or not, the impact of the offer would remain and stand us in good stead should the pitch stay postponed. A no-lose scenario.

# CHAPTER 9

# Anytime, anyplace, anywhere: the elevator pitch

If you had to summarise your pitch in a couple of paragraphs, could you? How the discipline of the elevator pitch is the basis of every great pitch.

The concept of the elevator pitch became famous during the so-called 'dot-com bubble'. In those days there was something of a feeding frenzy going on. Investors were keen to find hot new internet businesses to throw money at. Entrepreneurs were equally keen to pitch their wild ideas at investors, in the hope of becoming wildly rich and retiring at the age of 24 to a big house on a tropical island to enjoy a life devoted to tantric sex with supermodels. The theory was that any time might be pitch time, and often it was. The idea of the elevator pitch is simply this: should you ever find yourself in a lift with a potential investor, you would need to be able to have pitched to them by the time you reached the top floor. In a large skyscraper, maybe a couple of minutes.

## Today, you don't even have to be in the elevator

In the present day, we recently created an elevator pitch for ourselves, designed to run off an iPod. (In fact, any gadget with a screen, because the formats can be tailored to work on mobile phones, a BlackBerry and pretty much any other handheld media player.) It combines imagery, narrative and soundtrack. We did it for similar reasons to the dot-commers. Any time *could* be pitch time. We meet people at conferences, in bars, even socially at parties. There's nothing worse than finding out that one of your colleagues met a potential client by accident and didn't take the opportunity to pitch. And there always is an opportunity to pitch, without you even having to volunteer it. Nine times out of ten it will be when the question is asked, 'So what do you do then?'

**brilliant tip**

Adapting your credentials into mobile formats ensures focus and consistency and gives your elevator pitch viral potential. Modern communication tools mean you can give an elevator pitch and not even be present at the time.

The upside of the iPod format is that anyone in the company can fire up the gadget and give an instant elevator pitch. This way it is absolutely consistent, every time. You don't have to rely on somebody umming and aahing their way through some lame approximation of what your business does. Consistency is good. It means that every little enquiry can be met with an optimised pitch, from a senior director to the person who answers the phones (they meet people too). Mobile formats also deliver viral potential. It's easy to swap the file from phone to phone, and we find it a useful recruitment tool as well as a new business tool. It also makes your staff feel good about the company and what you do. Most people would rather tell a good story about the company they work for than a bad one. It has also had one other benefit: when we first started showing this to prospects they were blown away by it. For a company called Ingenuity it seemed so obvious that we needed to be ingenious about the tools we used to sell ourselves. (See page 174 for more on the subject of 'the medium is the message'.) Often, we would use it in preference to the dreaded PowerPoint deck, because after two minutes of scene setting we could get into what both parties really wanted to talk about – them, not us.

## Think about benefits, not features

The content is the tricky bit. It is by definition a non-tailored pitch and so the benefits will be generic. But what it does do is deliver the core message. Political parties could benefit from this. They tend to have 'policies' for everything, but of course nobody ever reads them (including their own people, half the time). What they generally lack is a simple, clear statement of what they stand for. This is usually assumed to be a 'given' and that people somehow automatically 'get' what they are about. Nothing could be further from the truth.

You should do an elevator pitch not only to acquire the benefits described above, but also to serve as a benchmark against which to judge any future pitch you may embark upon.

Doing an elevator pitch is not as easy as you might think. Coming up with a short summary has never been easy. As long ago as 1656, Blaise Pascal wrote (you can find it in his collection *Lettres provinciales*) that he had only written such a long letter because he had not had the leisure to write a shorter one. However, you should not take this to mean that you should start long and whittle it down. The way to do it is to start short and write it up. This is, after all, a process by which you need to bring out the bare essentials of your proposition. Who are you and what do you do? How are you demonstrably new, different or better? Why should anyone care? These are the kinds of questions you will have to address. In the case of the dot-com elevator pitch, the process is made easier by the fact that the audience definition is clear. Out of that fall the requirements of this particular audience, and out of that falls the content of the pitch. When it is more general, make some decisions. Select a likely target audience. I assume this will be

> you need to bring out the bare essentials of your proposition

potential customers. You can therefore make some good assumptions about what their priorities are, based on your knowledge of your current customers. The elevator pitch should match your features and benefits to their needs and requirements. As ever, stories can be a good way of communicating multiple messages in a memorable and impactful format. What are your stories – and what is *your story?* When you have matched what you offer to the usual requirements of most of your prospects, hopefully illustrated by a story or two, you will also need to consider the other dimension to your business – personality.

## Avoid the corporate 'personality bypass' operation

The 'people buy people' maxim is every bit as valid here as elsewhere in the pitch process. You have a personality (you do, don't you?) so let's communicate that. It is an asset. Some prospects will find it engaging and attractive. Others may be repelled by it. Trust me, both outcomes are valuable. Not everyone is a good match for everyone else – life simply isn't like that. Given the importance of personal chemistry in the buying process, it is as useful to find out that a prospect does *not* like you as to find out that they *do*. Companies have wasted endless amounts of time and money on pitches over the years that have failed due to simple lack of chemistry. If only they'd known that up front they could have simply chosen not to pitch at all in many instances. Your elevator pitch should tell it like it is, because the worst-case scenario is that you might avoid wasting lots of effort on a pitch that will ultimately go nowhere. That's a pretty good worst case. By being up front with your personality you may also attract buyers that might previously not have considered you, generating a new pitch opportunity in unexpected circumstances. By incorporating the personality of your business into the elevator pitch you will end up with something unique, rather than the kind of thing any of your competitors might have

> not everyone is a good match for everyone else

come up with. It will be a unique blueprint, the DNA of your own business.

Buyers generally don't like companies that lack personality. The personality is the thing that helps to bring features and benefits to life and creates the desire to do business with you.

## Telling a good story

So what should be in your elevator pitch? This is impossible to answer without knowing a lot about your company – each one should be unique. As a general rule of thumb, it again starts with putting yourself in the shoes of your audience. Assume they know nothing about you. You now have two minutes to get them from ground zero to being interested. What would turn you on? You'd need to know the basics about the company (facts and figures, how long established, turnover, employees, key skills, even small things like the location). You don't need to start with this, however. I would suggest you end with it.

Even a pitch to a very generalised audience needs to be focused on customer benefits, not corporate features.

Start instead where the prospect would like to start. And that's probably going to be focused on their challenge areas. So kick off with what you have achieved, and for who – make the success stories short and prominent, the customer endorsements loud and clear. Make it a brief and rapid sweep through a raft of successes (you may hopefully prompt further enquiry on the back of one of them – and then you are already armed with a clue as to what their needs are). Also talk about *how* you have achieved these successes – is there some process which underlies it, some methodology? Maybe it is a product-led pitch, so make them your heroes, but still focused on the *benefits* to the buyers. Prospects will not just want to know the generic benefits of what you do, but they will also, most importantly, want to know *why you?* Do you have better people? Do you have better processes? Do you have a better product, a killer application, a fabulous customer service record? Are you more environmentally friendly? Have you won awards for what you do? All of this is material that should make the cut. Be shameless, be proud of yourselves. And remember that your own staff are a significant part of the target audience for the output. Yes, they will want to hear that their own company is great, but they may be on the front line in that very first encounter, so they had better believe that what you've come up with is true! Any slight sign of scepticism will not go unnoticed.

What we end up with is a recipe that includes content, tone and style, and all of these must be as finely tuned to what you know about your audience as you can make them. If your elevator pitch is true to your business, it may help you better understand what attracted your customers to you in the first place. This is where the 'benchmarking' comes in. Your elevator pitch will have forced you to be very clear about your benefit story. It will have forced you to prioritise and maybe to exclude some of the more peripheral bits and pieces entirely. It will also force you to be clear about your audience and where they're coming from. This is a spectacularly useful exercise.

## Decide what you do (and what you don't do)

We have worked with agencies on many occasions where we have asked them to give us their elevator pitch. Often they can't. The worst examples are where an agency says, 'Well, we can help in lots of different areas.' This creates a pitching problem for us.

Buyers are seldom in the market for a company that can do a *range* of things; usually they are looking around because there is *one* thing that they need and they cannot get it from their incumbent. It's easy to sell a specialist service, but much harder to sell a generalist one. This discipline forces you to make decisions, identify priorities and strip out the non-essentials. More importantly, it focuses you on your customers. We then advise these businesses to go back and rethink what they really do. Often they will be thinking in terms of their own discipline – we do media, or digital, or PR, for example.

> it's easy to sell a specialist service, but much harder to sell a generalist one

In another market, an agency I once worked for advised a maker of DIY tools, mainly drills, to consider what business they were really in. Their view was that they were in the business of making drills. Not unreasonable you might presume. The agency's suggestion was that maybe they were in the business of making holes. The impact of that shift in perspective was dramatic. From a point of view that was self-centric, which completely came from them, they had moved to a customer-centric view of why they existed.

Having been through the elevator pitch process, and deciding what business we are really in, we at Ingenuity can run any pitch through the benchmark of the elevator pitch. It has helped us decide on some occasions to decline a pitch, because the prospect is just not an Ingenuity kind of client.

## Extrapolating the lessons of the elevator pitch process

The same disciplines can be applied to bigger pitches. What *are* the essentials, really? Are we focused on the need-to-haves, or are we getting distracted by the nice-to-haves? Have we got a clear fix on life as seen from the prospect's point of view, and do the key points we want to make address the same key issues they want to unpack? If you seem to be spending too much time in your pitch on stuff that didn't make the cut in the elevator pitch, this could be a warning sign that something has gone wrong. Perhaps you shouldn't even be doing the pitch at all. The businesses that do well at pitch are the ones that have a very clear idea of who they are and *therefore* why they are in the room at all.

If you find yourself working up a pitch that is not focused on the key material in your elevator pitch, you need to ask why. It may be that you are about to compete in areas that are peripheral to your business but may be core strengths of a competitor. In this instance you should decline the pitch. It may be that you have become distracted by the messages you are receiving from your prospect. Sometimes they can give you mixed messages, and you will have to decode them to work out what is really at the heart of the issue. Other times they may simply be being deliberately sparing in the amount of information they are prepared to release to you. If, however, your pitch had started from the point of the elevator pitch, and it was short, focused and to the point, you should already have a clear idea of what it was that was floating their boat.

# CHAPTER 10

# What to do when what they want is not the same as what they need

How to pitch to an audience that may not like what you have to say.

mongst the very first things I learned as a fledgling 'suit' in advertising were the two great dilemmas of account management. The first was this. A good account man would, like Janus, successfully navigate the problem of having to represent – simultaneously – both the client to the agency and the agency to the client. It's a classic intermediary, 'added value' role, although the real value-add would often lie in the skill of the individual in negotiation and the art of selling (to both sides). The *great* account man (and I would hasten to add that many of them were account women) would be able to pull off the feat of having each side in the debate believe that they were really, truly, deeply on *their* side. The worst place, of course, ever to be in was that of the individual incapable of persuading either side that they had their best interests at heart. For these poor creatures, a (short) career in advertising would consist of taking grief from both sides, all the time.

The second great dilemma was this: the simple fact that with many clients, what they *wanted* was often not what the agency felt they *needed*. Marketing directors might, for example, have a view of themselves and their brand as 'cool'; and yearn for ground-breaking advertising that would shift vast quantities of product *and* go down well at dinner parties at which they could claim the credit for the strategy. The challenge for the agency would be the grim reality that folk are not actually that turned on by breakfast cereals. Instead, a better strategy might just be to abandon the 'Hey! Breakfast is cool!' strategy and perhaps focus on the benefits of the 'It keeps you regular' strategy instead. A random, hypothetical example, but you get the point. Thankfully, most of this tends to be the day-to-day stuff of an ongoing client/agency relationship. It's exponentially harder to deal with when it crops up in a pitch.

## Risk and reward

In a pitch, you have a stark choice: do you take the easy route and go with what the prospect says they want, or do you take the high-risk route of telling them they're wrong and offering up what you think they need? In a pitch, you have one shot to get it right. Your answer to this question will automatically polarise your chances. You could choose to hedge, of course. Some will refuse to hedge their bets; they will go with their convictions. Others will accept the client viewpoint and stick with it. The worst position, I suggest, is that of the hedger. Marketing clients have told me over the years that the first people eliminated from the competition would be those that said, 'Yes, we could do this (and we'd be happy to!), or you could do something completely different (and we'd be happy to!). On balance, we'd probably recommend one over the other, but we'll go with whatever you decide (and we'd be happy to!).'

> the worst position is that of the hedger

There is no comfort here for any buyer. If you claim in any way, shape or form to be some sort of 'expert', you must at least do your prospect the courtesy of saying what your opinion is. Otherwise you are worthless.

If you've read earlier chapters (I hope you have), it would be apparent that you should not find yourself in this position in the first place. Maybe you would have taken control of the agenda at an early strategic discussion. Certainly your early 'engagement' strategy would have rooted this out way back in the process.

## Tackle it early – don't wait until the pitch

If you become aware of this want-versus-need dilemma early, there are various tactics you can adopt. The key, as ever, lies with the people on the other side of the table. Once you have diagnosed the situation, you can try the stealth challenge approach. Here, you simply use questioning to float the origins of your ideas subtly, without revealing where you are taking it. Make it part of the 'routine' questioning process you would always go through in the early stage of a pitch. Encourage them to ask themselves difficult questions. Play devil's advocate. See where you, and they, go with it. This should give you some early sense of the lie of the land.

I said the key to this lies in the people on the other side of the table; the first question you need to answer is, 'Are they unanimous?' The answer is more often 'no' than you might imagine. Different team members have different agendas – just as yours may do – and there may be shades of opinion that you can identify from early conversations. Perhaps things that have been said in the past now make more sense. It may be that they just genuinely aren't sure what the best course of action is – also common, and a very valid reason for calling a pitch – but, in this instance, they would probably have already come clean that they are open to various possible solutions. But this chapter is about what you do when this is *not* the case.

**brilliant** tip

If the want-versus-need dilemma is a genuine one, the chances are that there will already be some kind of internal split on the client side. Internal divisions often create opportunities.

If they are not unanimous, you need to work out how and why the team is split. You also need to work out who is on what side and how senior they are. You're probably not pitching to a democracy; someone will be the key decision maker and others will be the key influencers. You can also try to establish, from your attempts to float the initial stealth challenge, the temperature of the responses. Vehemently for or against? Non-committal? Open controversy? Look out for a potential internal champion. This would be someone who not only buys into your own way of looking at things, but also carries enough weight internally to be able to swing the opinions of others. Such a person might be worth investing in. In some cases, you might even contact them separately and share with them your observation that you both seemed to be on the same page, and your reservations about how the rest of the team feel about an alternative strategy. You can also emphasise the purity of your motives for the conversation. Make sure they understand that your concern is to come up with the best solution to the brief given and this involves exploring and, if necessary, eliminating all the other alternatives. That's a hard position to argue with. They may welcome your help. Even in the worst-case scenario, if you've misread it and they back off and tell the rest of the team about your conversation, you should still have no reason to be embarrassed about it. If they *do* buy into it, and you have enough time, you can work with them to help shape the outcome. You can, and should, do this in such a way that you could stand up in front of the most senior prospect and explain yourself with no hint of shame. If you do actually want to do the best job you can for your prospect, that motivation should hold you in good stead. It can surely be used to justify your efforts to explore the possibilities of bringing the prospect team on board with your thinking.

> look out for a potential internal champion

## Dealing with want versus need in a pitch

Sometimes, tackling the issue early is just not possible. You might have to pitch, with little chance to engage with anyone much beforehand, and do it on the day. This is a more frequent instance when dealing with intermediaries or consultants, to which the ultimate prospect might have outsourced the process. These people see part of their 'value' as being their ability to shield the prospect from the unwelcome attentions of a bunch of competing companies. Anything you share with them may or may not get passed on, but any feedback you get from them is unlikely to be much help to you. The role of the intermediary is to try to ensure a level playing field for the competitors. Your role is to give yourself an unfair competitive advantage.

So you're close to the pitch date, you have established the want-versus-need dilemma and you're stuck with it. What then? Step one is to try to do some sort of 'people audit'. Go back through what you know about the people in the pitch. Where do they come from? What did they do when they were there? (Were they revolutionaries or a safe pair of hands, or did they just bend with the wind and go with what their boss said?) Take a view on it. My gut feel would be to go with your gut feel – if you believe in something, it will come across at the pitch. If you're not sure, that will come across too.

The next step to consider is how to build a body of evidence in your favour. There are various ways you can do this. Third-party endorsement can be one. Is there an editor of a relevant trade publication you can float a hypothesis by? If they sound sympathetic (and they may also give you some good reasons *why* they are sympathetic that might not have occurred to you), this might carry some weight. Other people to approach might include non-executive directors or other industry experts (there are always industry experts to be had if you look hard enough).

**brilliant** tip

Your customer's customers can be your greatest asset in persuading an intransigent client to change their mind. Look for ways in which you can use them creatively to underpin your argument.

Do not forget your audience's audience. If what you are pitching is going to have any effect on your prospect's own customers then use that as the huge opportunity it is. I have seen many a prospect crumble when confronted by the voice of the consumer. And by voice, I mean voice. You could go out and do some 'research', but this would be expensive and would probably take a lot of time to organise, debrief and collate into a presentable format, and frankly you don't need it. What you do need is something that will do the job on the day. Instead, consider going out and actually talking to some customers, taking a video camera with you.

The 'vox pop' has proved a powerful weapon over many years in pitches. Even a hardened prospect will think twice when confronted by people they know to be actual customers (or potential customers) telling it like it is on camera. A montage (suitably edited) of customers agreeing with your point of view will be a powerful tool. I have seen pitches in the past where agencies have gone out on to the street, asked leading questions of random passers by, edited them like crazy and then presented the results as the verdict of Joe Public. It's pretty convincing – and much more impactful than presenting carefully crafted charts, graphs and other forms of data which might actually have some truth behind them. I'm not advocating that you lie – I'm simply advocating that you present a position in which you truly believe in its best possible light.

present a position in which you truly believe in its best possible light

Other evidence in favour of your argument might emerge from examining what your prospect's competitors are up to or are about to get up to. This might be gleaned from the trade press. (See discussion in Chapter 5 about the value of talking to industry journalists as a shortcut to finding out what's what.)

## Risk and reward – the prospect's perspective

You can also run 'what if' scenarios. What would be the consequences if your prospect did actually pursue their intended route? If you think it's wrong then see whether you can find ways to dramatise the consequences of that action. You will need to think creatively about this too. Perhaps data analysis is a way forward, or perhaps it is going to have to be a case of finding some 'expert witnesses' to act as advocates on your behalf. The big 'what if' is, what if they do it your way? It will help your case in presenting the upside if you can show that you have gone out of your way to look at the worst-case scenario that might arise from your approach. If it looks like the risk is not as great as may have been imagined, your case will be twice as strong. As with most selling, you have to consider how to remove the barriers to the sale as well as creating reasons to sign.

Your final weapon is you. If you opt to challenge the brief and pitch something you think they need but do not want then you absolutely have to sound like you mean it. Even if you don't think it's a risk, you are still asking them to shift their mental perceptions a long way in a short time and you need to be sympathetic to that. One of the reasons they might come along with you is the passion and conviction that is evident in your pitch. This is no time for half measures. And who are you anyway? (Meaning, why should I trust you?) Make sure that before you close with conviction, you open with some reasons why they might take your personal point of view very seriously. Their business might depend on it.

# CHAPTER 11

# Pitching for entrepreneurs: backing the rider or backing the horse?

How and why investors do, and don't, buy into ideas pitched to them. And what to do about it.

I t's a cruel irony that when entrepreneurs are pitching for investment, it's usually at the very time they are least capable of pitching for it successfully. The consequences of failure can be catastrophic, perhaps not merely ending a young company, but also ending someone's lifelong dream along with it. Young businesses often have young management teams – bright eyed and bushy tailed they may be, but all too often untried and untested in the real world of business. Furthermore, as a management *team* – and we'll come back to the importance of that later in the chapter – they are likely to be incomplete, lacking the breadth of skill set needed in a fully formed business. These gaps in the team's skills can quickly be exposed when pitching to investors, because success will require attention to a wide range of critical areas, spanning the entire breadth of the business.

Before getting into the process of pitching for funding, I would advise any entrepreneur to take a step back and think carefully about what they are trying to achieve. During my time as marketing consultant to the Software Business Network, a business growth service that was co-funded by the government, we spent an awful lot of time grooming entrepreneurs and talking to a wide range of investors, from large venture capital funds to individual 'business angels' (high net worth individuals looking to invest in early stage enterprises). One recurring theme was the need to make sure our entrepreneurs had thought through their answer to this question: are you sure you are seeking *the right funding, from the right people, at the right time?* This is a question that you will need to address, and it's certainly not something that a few pages of this book will be able to fix for you. You need sound advice tailored to your own unique situation.

## brilliant tip

You can't spend too much time researching your sources of funding, especially early stage. Get that right before you even think about writing a pitch.

## All funding is not the same

You need to take advice on the relative merits of where to go to get the right investment. Venture capital funding may or may not be right for you, and is probably only viable when your business is already some way down the road to success and requires fairly substantial sums to expand. In some sectors, notably high tech, businesses can be on their third or even fourth round of funding within the first five years. In the earliest stages of development, the business may be better suited to investment from 'business angels'. One advantage of this route is that a business angel can bring much more than just cash to the table. Angels typically invest in sectors they already know very well. As such they can offer you valuable advice about what works and what doesn't. They also bring something that could otherwise take decades to build – a Rolodex of valuable contacts both inside and outside your own industry, as well as their own personal introduction to them. They may have become high net worth individuals through running successful businesses of their own; they may have

> a business angel can bring much more than just cash to the table

managed large enterprises; they may have steered a small business right through to initial public offering (IPO). In short, they can be more than just investors – they can be an invaluable source of knowledge, wisdom and mentoring. Here too, just as there are different types of funding, there are also different types of business angel – some are happy to be involved and invest their time as well as their money, others are not. Decide what you want and make sure your understanding of how the relationship might work is a shared one.

Your pitch process will consist of four stages – namely:

- the preparation stage;
- writing the business plan;
- testing the plan;
- presentation.

## Preparing your pitch

In the preparation stage you will be putting together the basic components of your proposition. You will need to examine the various templates and business models that are available and work out which one fits your own business best. Don't try to force fit your own service business into a template designed for a manufacturing business, for example. There are plenty of places you can go to get advice, ranging from banks to trade associations, informal web-based social networks (most entrepreneurs are enthusiastic users of these), government-funded business advice sources, even specialist business incubators. You will need to get to grips with the fact that there will be a lot of things you need to learn and that it's going to take some time. You will need to learn how to write a business plan, how to evaluate a market, how to assess the strengths and weaknesses of your competitors and how to manage money. You will also have to learn 'softer' skills such as how to network. It's a big list. There are also some other things you will need to do, depending on your particular situation. You will need to set your own objectives (if you are one of the owners) and the company's objectives. You may need to write a strategic development plan and conduct activities like market research to back up your assumptions. You might also have to hire people, particularly if the business has some skills gaps. If you are a little more established, you might have to put in place a succession plan. Investors need to be clear about who's on board and how long they're going to stick around. This doesn't have to mean you're going to be tied in for ever, because investors also recognise that people need to have an exit plan. The main thing is that *there is a plan*, that it's out in the open and that everyone knows exactly where they stand from the outset.

## Writing and testing the business plan

Eventually, a first draft of the business plan will be written; if your plan is to withstand the trials of the pitch stage, it had better not be the only draft. Writing a business plan is not an event, it is an iterative process. Completing draft one simply means you can test it. My advice is, once again, to get help from people who have been there and done it – and ideally done it within your own industry. As you work through the plan with them, any holes in the logic should become apparent. Any overly optimistic assumptions will be challenged and picked up, and there may well be a few of those as it is always tempting to assume a favourable outcome over an unfavourable one. Any gaps in your knowledge should become clear too. Perhaps you're not as clued up about price elasticity as you thought, or maybe your marketing plan assumes an unrealistically high return on investment. You may need to bring in specialist help. Depending upon what the first interrogation reveals, help might be needed to deal with anything from

> writing a business plan is not an event, it is an iterative process

cash flow forecasting to pricing policy, to channel and distribution strategy. This feedback loop feeds the iterative process of testing and refining, so that over a period of time (and this could be two to three months) the weaknesses are eliminated. Another beneficial side effect is that it will embed many of the key facts, assumptions and metrics in your own head. This is also impressive to investors, who prefer to deal with people who 'know their numbers' rather than those who have to pause while they look them up.

Eventually your plan will be pitch-ready – and robust enough to satisfy both you and the people you have roped in to help you develop it. At which point I can tell you something that might make you think you've just wasted all that effort. (Trust me, you haven't.) Investors in early stage businesses – especially very early stage businesses – will enter the process on the basis that your business plan is a work of fiction. Educated guesswork it may be – well informed, researched and tested, and good enough to pass the intuitive radar of people with the experience and skills to pass judgement – but it's guesswork nonetheless. Until you have been in the market long enough to base a business plan on a track record of real world data, it cannot be anything else, can it?

## Investors focus on the people more than the plans

Syed Ahmed was a competitor on *The Apprentice* and went a long way in the competition. He ultimately missed out, if that's the phrase I'm looking for, on the peculiar thrill of working for Sir Alan Sugar. However, before long he was busy setting up a business of his own – SAVortex, a company which has designed and manufactured a unique type of hand dryer, using technology that is new to the market. It is (as described in detail within the business plan) technology that is 'greener', more effective, cheaper, longer lasting – it's even better from a health and safety point of view. I have got to know Syed quite well and spoke to one of his investors to find out how it came about that he had got involved in the business. It turned out that it wasn't entirely down to the business plan. Not that there was anything wrong with the business plan, far from it. It was rather persuasive, and it had also served its purpose in demonstrating an ability to produce such a document to the required level of quality. No. What had clinched the investment was the man himself. The innovative dryer technology was very interesting and the market projections attractive, but ultimately he'd placed his bet on his belief that Syed had what it takes to drive the business forward. If this surprises you in any way then think again. This was precisely the answer I had expected – because it almost always is. In early stage investment, and to a slightly lesser extent in subsequent rounds of funding, investors are *backing the rider, not the horse*.

## brilliant tip

Investors will prefer a great person with an average idea over an average person with a great idea, every time. You need to look even more convincing than your business plan.

Backing the rider, not the horse. So it's back to you again – or you and your team as the case may be. When the dragons in *Dragons' Den* come out with comments like 'I don't like you and I don't like your product, so I'm out', they're not just being nasty about it. (Mostly.) It is absolutely as much a professional observation as a business one. As an investor you've got to have a good feeling about the people who are going to be spending your money. Of course, investors will take a view on the business, but any serial investor will tell you that business plans are no substitute for business facts, and in the absence of years of good looking fact, it boils down to a judgement call on future potential rather than past performance. They will start by looking at what you have done to get to this point. They will also look at *how* you have got to this point; the simple act of seeking advice along the way (and, even better, taking it) will be a positive, not a negative. 'Well done,' they will think, 'they have the sense to know when they're not up to speed with something and to use their common sense to plug the gaps.' For any

> it boils down to a judgement call on future potential

investor it is reassuring to know that you are dealing with people who will call the lifeguard early, and not keep wading into ever deeper water while telling you everything's fine. Big tick.

## Does your team have what it takes?

In most cases, the investors will be taking a long hard look not at an individual, but at a management team. Your business plan can be as persuasive as Henry Kissinger, but if your management team doesn't look like it has the skills and experience to execute the plan, the investors have a problem. You have a problem. While you are interrogating your plan you should be asking yourself some tough questions about the human assets of your business. The upside is that this is usually something you can fix. The reason it is fixable is that when you are looking for gaps in your skills, the gaps are far more likely to be missing chunks than an overall weakness across the board. If it were across the board, you would have to get a whole new management team. 'Chunks' of skill can be patched in. You could buy in some consultancy, subcontract to a specialist business or hire people. Investors like teams with complementary skills, especially when the team is a small one. It's better to have three average people with completely different, complementary skills, than two brilliant people who do exactly the same thing. I have found this to be the case myself, when securing backing to start a digital agency. The backers liked the fact that the two principals were a good fit in terms of skills – a management guy with strategic and sales skills to run the business and a creative guy to ensure the quality of the end product.

> ## brilliant tip
>
> Don't get too hung up about the business plan at the expense of getting the right line-up of people. Whatever the plan says, it will be down to the people to deliver it, and the whole thing stands or falls on how confident your investors are in their ability to do that.

I have also found myself going through this process on the other side of the fence, when investing in a business. On this occasion, the situation was a pitch to a group of potential angel investors. The business plan looked good, I bought their assumptions, the numbers stacked up, I liked the prognosis and it all felt believable. So far so good. The ability to make things happen in the real world is what counts, however. My decision was made on the basis of two things. First, I took account of the opinions of my fellow business angels (all of them, unlike me, 'serial investors'). Second, I took account of my own gut feel and intuition. The deciding factor was the quality of the management team and their performance in the pitch. They certainly knew their stuff (they had been through the test/refine process, so not only did the answers exist, but they also had them at their fingertips). They were very confident when fielding questions from the floor, and the answers they gave were measured and credible. They were not trying to second-guess us by giving us the 'right answer', which is good because there is only ever one right answer – the honest answer. They were also able to explain in some detail how the management team proposed to work as a team, how the roles and responsibilities were divided up and the relevant experience of each of the team members in relation to their role. There were some weaknesses in certain areas, but the particularly encouraging aspect of this was that these weaknesses weren't discovered as a result of close questioning – they were volunteered. Furthermore, there was a plan in place to address the knowledge gaps. All of this was explained in a clear, calm and structured way. There was a good level of passion in evidence, balanced with evident professionalism. In the discussions afterwards we all agreed that not only was this a bunch of people with a good plan, but also, more importantly, a bunch of people we felt were capable of putting the plan into action. The entrepreneurs got their money, and they continued to get money through subsequent funding rounds. The faith of the investors was repaid handsomely when the business was sold to a large trade buyer a few years later.

# CHAPTER 12

# Victory is not about coming up with the right answer

Why, in the creative and media world, the work done for a pitch seldom sees the light of day. Why this matters and how to frame your pitch accordingly.

An agency friend of mine won an advertising pitch recently. I asked him when the work was due to go live and he told me, but he added that the work that was going to appear was not actually what was presented in the pitch. The work that had won the pitch had been ditched by the client. They were going to go with something else. Now this is a conversation I have had many times; a scenario frequently repeated. Creative work is presented in a pitch environment, one agency wins, but the pitch-winning work is then abandoned in favour of something different. What can we learn from this?

## Direction versus destination

In these scenarios, the buyers have clearly taken the view that something else outweighs the quality of the pitch work. So, what might that be? Well, it in part goes back to the 'people buy people' thesis. The winning agency has been chosen not because it came up with the right answer (clearly, it didn't), but because it was deemed to be the agency *most likely* to come up with the right answer. For people selling service propositions, or consultative propositions, this is particularly important. If you choose to see the pitch as an opportunity to showcase yourselves and your working methods, rather than make the output the hero, you end up running a different sort of pitch. And you still stand as much chance of creating pitch-winning work.

The issue here is direction versus destination. Sometimes, you have a prospect that (to borrow a cliché from a previous US presidential campaign) has some sense of 'the vision thing'. However, although they feel they are on a journey, the prospects are unsure about exactly how to get there, or even what the final destination may be. The early clue for the competitors is when the brief is either vague or ridiculously uncertain. For ad agencies, it's rarely helpful for clients to issue a brief that is couched in broad, sweeping terms – but lacks real world, hard-edged rationale to back it up. All you're left with is heroic-styled advertising with no factual underpinning, and that will just be a big waste of the client's advertising budget. No pitch is going to work unless the buyer and seller have a *shared vision*. Buyers need a clear understanding of what they're buying and sellers must have a clear understanding of what they're selling. Sounds obvious, doesn't it?

> no pitch is going to work unless the buyer and seller have a *shared vision*

## Productising early stage sales

Let me illustrate this from the angle of someone trying to sell in a big 'blue-sky concept' to buyers who might well need the benefits being promised, but are uncertain about how to get there. In this case, the agency (let's call it Lemon) had a proposition eminently capable of getting them in front of buyers, but they couldn't close the deal. The whole thing was stalling at the first meeting. There was seldom a second meeting. Lemon's ultimate objective was to work with brand owners, to develop new ways of communicating with consumers through content-led techniques.

To buyers, complexity equals risk, and when the benefits are hard to quantify up front the perceived risk increases exponentially. You will need to unpack the process into smaller components to de-risk it.

Lemon's idea was good. It was aligned with the way the market was moving and they were ahead of the trend. Eventually we were able to work out the problem and described it using the following short story.

Let's say I walk into a pet shop, I've been lured in, and my start point is that I fancy buying a parrot. The shop owner tells me they're out of parrots and actually nobody wants parrots any more. He says it's all about big cats nowadays – pumas, tigers, maybe even a lion. OK, I'm curious. I might like a lion.

I ask whether he's got a lion in stock, but he hasn't. I ask what it will cost, but he says it depends, because they're all individually priced. OK. So now I ask how long it might take if I order one, and again he's not sure because it depends on which country it comes from.

By now I'm going off the idea, and in any case, I'm also not sure what the family would have to say about it when I get home. Tempting . . . but I leave.

This is precisely what had been happening with Lemon. Having done the hard part, namely creating a level of desire, the buyers weren't buying and so there was never any action.

The reasons were these. While the end benefits were unusual and potentially exciting, the *duration* of the process of getting there was uncertain, so were the *costs* and so were the eventual *outcomes* and *benefits*. People were dropping out of the buying cycle at the evaluation stage, and a big part of that was the fear of having to justify a 'buy' decision to their boss, based on not enough information about the cost, the timing, the sort of big cat they'd end up with and what it would actually do for them.

The problem was the evaluation stage, and the solution was to break this up into smaller, bite-sized chunks.

The alternative ending of the pet shop story goes like this. As I'm about to walk away, the pet shop owner turns to me and says, 'I can tell you're tempted. Actually, I've got a small wildcat in the back room – you can take it away right now, it'll cost £100 and you can try it out. I'll come round in a month or so to see how you and your family are getting on with it and, who knows, maybe we can talk about a lion next.' In this scenario the pet shop owner has simply offered me a way to take the first step on the journey. A step I can take right now, at a fixed price, which will help me make a decision about the next step.

When you are pitching something big, hairy and scary (like a lion) the evaluation stage in the IDEA cycle is going to be a sticking point, especially if there are a lot of unknowns in there. One option is to 'productise' the early stages of the purchase process. This gives you the chance to get your customer on the road and, just as importantly, enables you to build a relationship during this short early phase. The ensuing relationship will prove invaluable as you guide the prospect through the purchase cycle to the ultimate goal. Buyers like to buy from people they know and trust. The purpose of this pitch is not to sell the lion today, it's to sell the lion tomorrow.

> buyers like to buy from people they know and trust

## The perception of risk

For many buyers, the real agenda is risk reduction. It may be timid, it may be downright cowardly, but it's out there. We've all done it. How many times have you bought something having weighed up various considerations and come down on the side of the option that is simply least likely to come back and bite you? Risk reduction. Insurance is a good example. I'll search for the cheapest quotes online, but I don't buy the cheapest quote. That would be some company I've never heard of and feels risky. So I'll end up buying a quote about a third of the way up the list, because I'll take the view that if something bad happens and I make a claim, I might actually get reimbursed. I'll decide to pay that little bit extra just in case. I may be completely wrong. There may be nothing wrong with the cheapest company. But it makes me feel a little better, and it's cost me extra so I have an extra excuse to feel secure. Buyers don't always have 'cheapest' as their ultimate criterion. Buyers sometimes need to feel they will be supported on the journey.

## Build in some flexibility

The journey is the next point I want to make. If your pitch is fully formed, costed and shaped as your 'final offer', for your buyer there are only two options: take it or leave it. That's quite a decision you are asking them to make in your pitch – would you make it if you were in their shoes? Would you not prefer an option that shares the journey, that has some room for manoeuvre, that gives you (not to put too fine a point on it) some room for covering your own back? No? Well you're a very brave person and I salute you. Meanwhile, for the vast majority of people you will be pitching to, life is not so simple. Let's see what we can do to help them.

If you offer a solution *and* some flexibility to reassess that sol-ution going forward, do you think a buyer is more, or less, likely to say yes? Well, what would you do? You're going to have to go back and justify your decision to someone higher up in the organisation (or even if not, you'll have some explaining to do if you bought the wrong thing). So, if you can go back with not only an answer but also a chance to reconsider built in, that's going to make you look like you made a smart decision. This dramatically reduces your buyer's perception of risk, even if your buyer has a pretty strong opinion that they got it right and won't need to reconsider anyway.

So what we've seen here is various buyer risk-reduction strategies in action. From the buyer that hires an agency not for the work delivered at the pitch – but because they believe the agency is best placed to work with them to *eventually* come up with the best work – to simple folk like me who don't buy the cheapest insurance quote because of the perceived risk of the insurer not delivering the ultimate benefit – paying out without fuss when a claim is made. All very human.

## The perception of value

A lot of this is about perception of risk, rather than a real, measurable analysis of risk. This is because (surprise!) buyers are human. Human beings perceive risk based not solely on fact but also on instinct. Plug into that and you can hot-wire yourself into your buyer's comfort zone. Robin Wight, the 'W' in London advertising agency WCRS, has for some years been an advocate of the need for advertisers to understand, and benefit from, the workings of the human brain as revealed by discoveries in the fields of psychology and neuroscience. Robin Wight is a very clever man. In an address to the organisation Arts & Business in 2007, he talked about the 'peacock's tail'. He suggested that one of our hard-wired reflexes is a favourable response to anything that is 'over-engineered'. I will oversimplify this as follows. His idea is that it has been established that the quality of the peacock's tail is a signal to a prospective mate of the fitness of a particular male. The level of resource needed to

> human beings perceive risk based not solely on fact but also on instinct

produce something as enormous, and otherwise gratuitous, as a peacock's tail tells the peahen that her genes stand a much greater chance of being passed on by mating with this particular, splendidly endowed peacock than the other, less impressive specimens that may be courting her. He went on to talk about the 'handicap principle'. This tells us that there must be a *cost* attached to the behaviour to ensure the signalling comes across as *genuine*.

He then applied this principle to marketing. I believe you can apply it to pitching too. What's happening here is the peahen is applying a hot-wired response to her own need to reduce the risk in mating with a male individual. She's using it to construct her own perception of risk and reward. Buyers do the same thing. There are signals you can show that will help your buyer feel reassured about the risk. What's your peacock's tail? It will need to have a cost attached – that's the impressive thing about the peacock's tail – and it will need to offer some benefit to your prospect. I would suggest that this should be a feature aligned with the process of ensuring your buyer will end up with the most appropriate solution. It could be a measurement or evaluation tool that you offer at your own expense – with luck, one that you need to deploy only scarcely during your relationship. It might be some other tool that reduces buyer risk, or contributes to the continuous improvement of your product or service. If you have these things already, move them forward and make a virtue of them; if you don't, you should consider what you might create.

## brilliant tip

Sellers like to talk about shared reward. Buyers like to talk about shared risk. By offering up a way of addressing shared risk that has a cost attached, a seller is sending a powerful message to the buyer.

These techniques are valuable because they reduce the risk, or more pertinently the perception of risk in the mind of the buyer. The pitch scenario in which they are of *most* relevance is the one where your product or service is not cast in stone. If you will be working alongside the prospect, if you may need to develop your offering over time or if the prospect is in any way unclear about the precise shape of the required solution, you are about to embark upon a journey with your buyer. In which case this is a need-to-have, not a nice-to-have. There is one other technique to consider, which will also help you to convince a buyer that you are the best partner to accompany them on the journey.

## Go on, make me laugh

Let's say I'm organising a function and I want to hire a comedian. I interview two comedians. The first one tells me about previous experience, has some references and is absolutely insistent that he is, within that glorious universe of comedians, an occupant of the highest celestial sphere of the comic universe. He sits (or so it would appear) at the right hand of Coco the Clown. So far so good, I'm cautiously impressed. A convincing and forthright pitch by someone not short on confidence. Comedian number two takes a different tack. He tells me straight away that while he has references, endorsements and experience that he can recite, he's not going to tell me about that. He understands, he explains, what it's like when you're looking to hire a comedian. Comedy, he says, is about making people laugh. So he tells me a joke, and another, and another . . . I have now made my decision, because I'm laughing. We can discuss the audience and the material later, the main thing is he's *funny*. I have that on the best possible authority – my own.

What he's done to me is quite simple. It's something you can do in your own pitch. He's dramatised not his solution, but his understanding of my problem. I can tell him about random relatives, their likes and dislikes, and the weak points of various colleagues that he can exploit for comedic value. But he gets the fact it's about making people laugh. The clients who hire agencies and then get them to produce different work from their pitch work are doing the same thing. They have bought into the agency as fellow traveller.

# CHAPTER 13

# Pitching to procurement professionals

How this audience requires a different approach and how to win them over.

f you were to ask a group of procurement professionals how they are viewed, you would get a mixed bag of answers, and I suspect not many of them would be heart-warming. Perhaps you don't care. Perhaps you'd rather attend a singles' night at the Institute of Actuaries in preference to spending time with procurement people. If we are to stand any chance of dealing with procurement people, we first have to understand them. And 'understood' is one thing procurement people are not.

Internally, they are often viewed as a 'necessary evil' and occupy the same mental pigeonhole as such things as plaster casts – they perform a useful function, but the process is tiresome and frustrating, and everyone's glad when it's over. Externally it's worse. Externally, they often fall into the '*un*necessary evil' category. Not only is the process acutely painful, but the accusation is that procurement people end up buying the wrong thing anyway, because, like Oscar Wilde's cynic, they know the price of everything but the value of nothing.

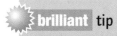 **brilliant** tip

Procurement people are like dentists. Visit regularly and you'll suffer only minor discomfort. It's only when you stay well away that it's painful when you do finally meet.

This view reaches its apogee amongst agency people. Most of them will run a mile rather than get involved with procurement. One criticism is that the further away you move from commoditised, simple products towards complex, value-added services, the less easy it is to compare like with like. Furthermore, the differentiating factors are, increasingly, the less tangible ones – factors related to the talent, skills and experience of human beings. Often, the criticism is more simply put. 'They just don't "get" what we do!' is what I usually hear, inevitably followed by a tirade about how bean counters can't possibly understand the subtleties and intricacies of creativity and have no business being allowed to buy a creative service anyway. This, I think, is an absolutely splendid opinion and long may it persist. It gives those of us who take the view that we should actively embrace procurement people a huge competitive advantage.

## Procurement – the industry that won't stay in its box

As we know, perception and reality are often two different things and this is particularly true of procurement. Furthermore, the reality of procurement is changing at a pace. When we first started inviting procurement people to events to meet with creative agencies, the knowledge levels of the attendees varied wildly. Some knew next to nothing about marketing (and freely admitted it). Others had a good working knowledge, while a few really did know a great deal about the agency world, right down to which ones were at the top of their game right now and which were struggling. A lot of them reported that their marketing colleagues were keen that they should 'stay in their box', whereas others had actually been recruited from the marketing and agency world. Poachers can, as everyone knows, make very good game keepers. The mar-

> the reality of procurement is changing at a pace

keting people, like the agency people, had a view that they knew best and that procurement people didn't understand the 'touchy-feely' side of the business, and never would. This was a primary driver in procurement people coming along to meet creative agencies. They came along to see for themselves what the big mystery was. A few years on, we see a very different kind of procurement professional emerging. There are still inconsistencies in knowledge, but I sense a growing self-confidence; a belief that they *do* have something of value to bring, that gaps in knowledge can be filled, and filled quickly, and that marketing and agency people need to understand that *they* can learn something from the disciplines of procurement. This is widely held to be a horrifying new development.

But it's not. The commonly held myth about procurement folk – that they don't 'get' people, creativity or grey areas – is breaking down. The procurement people who come along to meet agency people are doing so because they know that in order to do their job better, they do need to have a better understanding of issues that cannot always be reduced to a mathematical algorithm. Believe it or not, an increasing number of them do realise that whereas some things are so commoditised that you can run an internet auction and automatically award the contract to the lowest bidder, not everything can be bought in this way. A different approach is needed when buying a service capable of adding value to a business through the power of a creative idea. Where you find creativity, you find people and grey areas. You will also find procurement people ready to listen.

## The unexpected objectives

Did you know that the Chartered Institute of Purchasing and Supply (CIPS) has a Royal Charter? OK, so it's obvious. The clue is in the name. The surprising part is that one of the primary objectives of this fine body is this: 'To promote and develop for the public benefit *the art and science* of purchasing and supply, and to encourage the promotion and development of *improved methods* of purchasing and supply in all organizations.' (My italics.)

'Procurement is as much an art as a science.' 'Procurement practices are capable of improvement.' Both of these statements would figure rather high up in the list of utterances most people would never expect from a procurement person. The problem is that, from the outside, procurement people are seen as set in their ways. They make the Pope's version of 'infallibility' seem a little wishy-washy by comparison. So the commitment to the development of improved methods is both unexpected and welcome. It is also an opportunity. Then there is art. The art of the early Florentine masters of the trecento. The art of the postmodern movement. The art of feng shui, even. But the art of *procurement?* The use of the word 'art' is striking, and it will present us with our third opportunity. That science alone, by their own admission, is not the sole means of finding the best solution.

And so there you have it. Three opportunities to tackle procurement people with some hope of persuading them – rationally – of the merits of your point of view over and above a predetermined, fixed methodology. Two are enshrined in the Royal Charter of CIPS and one is a self-evident truth about how people interact.

### brilliant tip

Procurement people are commonly held to be intransigent. Like any negotiation, you won't get far without a proper understanding of what they are trying to achieve.

The concept of continuous improvement means that in a procurement pitch you can suggest that you might have a new and more effective way of shedding light on a difficult area. Sometimes you have to take a step back to move forward, and a useful tactic might be to suggest going back to re-examine the original objectives and then see whether the mechanism they currently have in place is the best way of delivering against those objectives. If you can find a flaw in it, you can put forward an alternative that works in your favour and trumps the previous mechanism. That would actually be a win-win scenario and might appeal to an ambitious audience.

## The art of measurement

'Art' allows us to talk for the first time within a procurement-led pitch about things that we intuitively know are important but are difficult to measure. Just because something can't be measured doesn't mean it's not important. The problems tend to come when procurement people are asking what you consider to be the wrong question, and frequently it's a question about measurement. They may want to measure hours spent – but you may want to be judged against the quality of output, not the quantity of time input. If that output happens to be something very hard to measure for whatever reason then it's going to be difficult to resolve the situation in your favour. There is a tendency in business to take comfort in things that can be measured, and sometimes it ends up with the tail wagging the dog. The same is true with governments, who like measuring things (especially things that can deliver good PR headlines) but sometimes find that the mindless pursuit of targets can create undesirable outcomes.

If a procurement person wants you to quantify something that is not quantifiable, you need to change the agenda. The way to do it is by suggesting an alternative as a more effective means of achieving the same end. If you try hard enough, there will always be a way of measuring X, however intangible X appears to be. Sometimes it might be measuring symptoms of its presence – X might have various side effects that are more easily measurable (customer satisfaction levels perhaps). I worked with a company once that measured things like the number of sick days taken by its staff, as an indicator of the level of the company's internal morale. 'Morale' is hard to measure, but the symptoms are more easily available. When there are a number of these, they can be woven into a surprisingly convincing web of indirect measurement.

If X is proving particularly elusive, and you cannot measure its presence, you can try measuring its absence. Cold, for example, is the absence of heat. If you think of a business as an ecosystem then, like any ecosystem, when something is missing it will cause a knock-on effect elsewhere. The absence of sufficiently good staff training might, for example, be the cause of a high number of items being returned by customers as being unsuitable for their needs. The symptom is more measurable than the disease. By identifying and measuring the knock-on consequences of absence, it is sometimes possible to create new metrics that actually suit both parties better.

Fortunately, procurement pitches rarely call for such extreme measures. Most times, you can actually navigate successfully through a pitch to procurement people by doing what I suggested in the first place – seeking them out and actively embracing them. As I've already suggested, you'll already be a step or two ahead of many of your competitors. Seek them out. They're not expecting it.

## brilliant tip

Procurement people like information and they like to get it in a certain way. Be proactive and get it over to them ahead of any request.

## The 'RFI in a box'

The first step in engaging with procurement people, and then shaping them to match your point of view, is to make contact. This should be done very early in the pitch process – ideally even before the formal pitch process has started. I recommend to clients of my company Ingenuity that they proactively seek out procurement people. Not surprisingly, their phones tend to ring a lot less than their marketing colleagues. This is perhaps one reason why they are more in the habit of answering the phone when it rings (as compared with the perpetual voicemail you find in marketing departments). A good early step is to make an effort to make their life easier. One way of doing this is to supply them with the kind of information they require in the long-listing stage *before* they actually get to the long-listing stage. If you've filled in a few PQQs (pre-qualification questionnaires) or RFIs (requests for information) or any of the other TLAs (three-letter acronyms) you find in business, you'll have spotted that most procurement people tend to ask similar questions. Size of business, key services, age of the business – in fact a whole raft of standard questions. It's a relatively easy task to recycle this information, package it up yourself and proactively supply it to your procurement targets in a ready-made form. Even if subsequently you have to do it again in their own format, you may find that the simple act of sending what we call an 'RFI in a box' has contributed to you being put on the list in the first place.

## When stress is good

Then go out of your way to court them. Earlier on in this chapter I suggested that procurement people are ready to listen. First, you must do some listening yourself. If you are to stand any chance of creating a constructive relationship with procurement, it is essential that you understand not just what they want, but also – more importantly – *why* they want it. If you don't have a clear understanding of their motivations, you might as well pack up and go home because you will never get them to shift their ground on anything. You need to listen hard to what's being said – not because you have any interest in how the forms need to be filled in, but because you are looking for holes, little flaws in the logic. Like tiny stress fractures in the wing of an airliner, with a little extra pressure they can suddenly open up and bring the whole thing crashing down.

> you are looking for holes, little flaws in the logic

One thing to look out for is any sign that a procurement process originally designed for a wholly different situation has been adapted for use in yours. This might give you the chance to exploit a small stress fracture and open it up. If not, continue to do what they say, but don't be afraid to challenge any assumptions you don't agree with. The trick is to pitch it as simply a different means to the same end. One assumption open to challenge, particularly when you are pitching higher value services, consultancy or similar, is the concept that lower price can be achieved without higher risk. Years ago, people I knew who worked for a technology company used to tell me that a good way to take on a 'difficult' procurement person was the tactic known as FUD; fear, uncertainty and doubt. Even a really brazen procurement person isn't going to welcome exposure to excessive risk simply to achieve a rock-bottom price. The question is, where exactly are the areas of risk and what are the possible consequences? So tell them.

## Re-calibrating what's important

Remember the 'RFI in a box' idea? You weren't thinking of *just* recycling a previous RFI, were you? No, this is a far more *creative* task. You will know what the strengths of your own company are, as well as the strengths and weaknesses of whatever it is you are pitching. You will also have a pretty good idea about how well you compare against your usual competitors. There are going to be some areas where you beat the others. (If you can't think of any, you might want to consider moving to another job.) Your task is to convince the procurement people that these are the areas that are critical to success. You also need to convince them that the absence of these strengths would increase the risk factor exponentially. This needs to be done as early in the process as possible, and that very first approach to procurement, even prior to the long-listing stage, is the ideal time to do it. And so your own 'RFI in a box' is not just a rehash of the standard questions you've answered in the past – it is an opportunity to create new questions, answer them forcefully in the affirmative and explain exactly why your company has made this a top priority.

*Question 14(b):* Does your company have NXV174 programming skills in-house?

*Answer:* HippityHop Industries has NXV174 programming skills both in-house and in depth. HHI is fully aware of the critical need for these skills, the essential nature of their contribution to the success of a project and the extreme risks presented by failure to have them either in-house or in sufficient quantity. HHI therefore retains a staff of 14 technicians fully skilled in NXV174.

The procurement person might not have the foggiest idea what NXV174 is. But it just might be enough for them to conclude that they ought just to check that all the contenders do have it. And how fabulous would that be, to get back a tender invitation six months later which makes a point of asking you about your own particular strengths?

**CHAPTER 14**

# Busking it: how to pitch without a pitch

The gentle art of *not* making it up as you go along, and how logic can be your best friend.

I t takes effort in preparation to come across as effortless in delivery. Comedians know this. A good stand-up comedian (especially the 'observational comedy' variety) can make you feel like they're just telling you stuff as it pops into their head. The material is carefully crafted and honed, but it often feels like stream of consciousness – even though as an audience we all know that it's been rehearsed. In a business pitch it is entirely possible to achieve the same effect, and you should make this your mission for one key reason – the more effortless your delivery appears to be, the more your audience will believe you to be the master of your subject.

In a normal pitch scenario, this isn't too hard to do, because you know in advance what you're going to say and why. But there are times when this is not possible and you find yourself suddenly having to make an impromptu pitch. When this happens, and you have to pitch without a pitch, you may need to resort to what we call 'busking it'. In real life we do this all the time, but don't notice.

## You need to get your brain organised

If a friend invites you to explain what's so great about your own football team then you're pitching. You'll probably do a half-decent job because you will be familiar with the material you're going to use to make the case. You may think you're busking it, and in one sense you are – by assembling material you are already familiar with into an impromptu pitch. In business, the chances are that you will be familiar with your own material, at least to the same extent as you are with your own football team.

### brilliant tip

For most people in an impromptu pitch situation, their biggest problem is not that they lack knowledge, but that they lack the means to *organise* it – and to retrieve it in a way that is flexible, relevant and seemingly effortless.

So why do so many people struggle when they have to pitch unexpectedly? It is not usually down to lack of knowledge. People struggle with impromptu pitches because they lack a mechanism to organise their existing knowledge into new patterns on the hoof. In Chapter 9 the subject of the elevator pitch was tackled. Sometimes this will be enough to get you through, but at other times it won't.

A designer found herself in front of a very tough and sceptical prospect in an office on Wall Street. The prospect was a highly successful female CEO of a financial services business. (So terrifying is she that she still smokes in her office; no underling has yet had the temerity to make any comment about this.) The topic under discussion was the firm's logo. The prospect was not at all convinced that logos made any difference to anything and had agreed to meet the designer largely for the amusement value she expected to derive from the encounter. The designer had been summoned at very short notice, had not had time to prepare and knew only that she was going to have to 'talk about the logo'. This was certainly going to be a case of busking it.

On arrival the prospect stubbed out another long cigarette and simply said, 'So, tell me about my logo.' The designer was able to do this. She was able to do this, from cold, for exactly the same reasons that I can pitch my business to anyone, any place, any time. It's by using a tool kit. The tool kit consists of an elevator pitch containing the components of a general summary of positioning, features and benefits. There are, however, two other crucial tools, beyond the elevator pitch, and these are the tools that make it possible for you to pitch without a pitch.

## Building your asset banks

The first tool is a mental asset bank of stories that illustrate various key points. The second tool is an asset bank of stock answers to the usual objections that may be raised, also in the form of short stories. These components can be assembled in any order, based on the angle the prospect is coming from, and when delivered sound like they're off the cuff despite the fact they've been pre-prepared. Not only will this make you more effective, but it will also make you more relaxed because you will know you are equipped to busk your way through pretty much any pitch scenario. The simple knowledge that you have your tool kit in your head has an automatic, beneficial effect on self-confidence. Anyone can do this, if you're prepared to be prepared. You see 'busking it' is *not* 'making it up as you go along'. It is the opposite.

> 'busking it' is *not* 'making it up as you go along'

The use of stories is important. Stories are how people remember, and to be an effective busker you will use stories to help you remember your own material. Your audience also needs to be able to remember. The greatest storyteller of all time, Jesus, used parables, which are highly memorable and have powerful messages embedded within them. I'm sure you can remember some of them. The memory effect is important when you find yourself in an unexpected pitch situation, because it's very possible that your audience is as unprepared as you are. They may not have pen and paper at the ready. When you go away you need to have given them a means to recall what you have been trying to communicate. If your key messages are buried in a fog of detail your chances of a successful result are diminished.

## brilliant tip

The ability to tell great stories is the key to success in unexpected pitch situations. Stories will help you and your audience to remember and turn information into communication.

When I have to talk about how an outsourced new business consultancy is required when the client already has a business development person, I don't go through a list of benefits. Instead, I tell a 'before and after' story about a real business development person. I talk about how he worked previously and how he works now. It also means I can talk about the benefits in emotional terms, which makes it more powerful and more memorable. I can talk about how he enjoys his job more and feels hugely more motivated now that he can focus exclusively on hot prospects, rather than worry about drumming up leads from cold to feed the pipeline. I can also talk about how even the finance director has acknowledged that the extra cost is more than repaid by the far greater return on the investment. When you can overlay a human spin on to a rather impersonal list of business benefits, the impact is amplified immeasurably.

Once you have broken down your key messages into bite-sized chunks, you can work out what stories you are going to tell to illustrate the points. Here is one example. I never talk about how we 'schedule highly qualified new business appointments with senior level decision makers'. Our competitors always say that, and it's really no more than should be expected anyway. But I know for a fact that that's not always the way it goes in the real world. Often, the meetings that are set are not qualified well enough. Instead, therefore, I relate the story of what it's like to be sent up and down the country, having spent half a day preparing for the meeting, probably to some inaccessible hell-hole supposedly to meet a marketing director, only to find out you're actually meeting someone who is one up from the biscuit boy ... (delivered now with increasing exasperation) and the first thing he says to you is, 'So, tell me why you're here?' They always relate to that, and they like the fact that somebody gets that it has an impact on them personally as well as professionally.

Meanwhile back in Wall Street, the next question asked of our designer by the prospect was an unexpected one. She reached under the desk and brought out a shopping bag, from Saks Fifth Avenue. 'Tell me about this logo,' she asked. The designer was able to do this too. She was able to do it by drawing analogies with other designs – ones cherry-picked from her mental asset bank of illustrative stories. There was a story about colour. A story about the power of typography. A story about how people react to different design cues. It sounded very compelling, it sounded as though the designer was giving specific answers to a specific question, but she wasn't. But it did have the effect of convincing the sceptical prospect that here was a person who absolutely knew what she was talking about.

The second tool, an asset bank of objection handling, is easy to shortlist. The same objections from buyers will crop up again and again, and the most common ones can be singled out to go into your asset bank. If you stick to the

**the same objections from buyers will crop up again and again**

top six, you should be able to cover off most eventualities. Again, if you can find a way to turn them into stories, they will have more impact. You could make a very short case study, based on a customer who shared that objection initially but has since changed their mind. You might want to consider using customer endorsements, opinions from third parties – anything that will help to bring the point to life and stick in the mind.

## Post-it notes

When you have your asset banks prepared, you can think of the stories contained within them as Post-it notes. Ideally you would have perhaps six stories that sell the main features, with a similar number that address the main objections. The elevator pitch is the hub around which they all revolve. Imagine that each Post-it note has the name of one story upon it. You would be able to pick them up and put them down in a different order as many times as you like. Try doing it mentally and see whether you can visualise each story and change the order. If you can do that, you've got everything you need to tackle the unexpected pitch opportunity.

## Use questioning to create a structured conversation

Your final tactic, although this may not always be possible, is to use questioning to help you structure your pitch and also buy time to think about the answers. By forcing your audience to think through their issues and needs in a logical sequence, you can order your own thoughts along the same structure. The process here is our old friend the cone. You will start with the broader issues and the bigger, contextual questions. You can then gradually drill down to identify the specific needs of the prospect and the context in which you will need to frame your answers. If you have your asset bank ready, it is then very easy to slot in the right story at the right time as you go along. This then begins to turn the situation away from being a monologue into a structured conversation. This is going to work harder for you, as the prospects will feel like they have played a part in the process of finding an answer. The asset bank will play a big role in making the process feel conversational. So, using an earlier example, if

> the asset bank will play a big role in making the process feel conversational

your prospect has a problem with being sent to poorly qualified meetings by a dodgy new business consultancy, the correct response is not to tell them that you 'schedule highly qualified new business appointments with senior level decision makers'. The correct response is to tell them the biscuit boy story.

You see what I did there? I bet you know what I mean when I refer to the 'biscuit boy' story from earlier in this chapter, and I suspect you could tell the story back to me. I also wouldn't mind betting that you had already forgotten the phrase 'schedule highly qualified new-business appointments with senior level decision makers'.

## Practice builds confidence

Confidence is, of course, a key component in being able to pitch, and particularly when you're not prepared for it. By rehearsing your asset bank stories you will never need to feel lacking in confidence in such a situation. That will give you an advantage straight away. There are occasions when a pitch can come at you from left-field, and it may be that it has caught you completely off guard. A design agency friend told me that she and the agency's founder occasionally used to throw junior people in at the deep end in pitches. In one instance, the junior person had been closely involved in the pitch process and therefore knew all he needed to know about the pitch. On the day, immediately before the actual pitch, his senior colleagues announced that he was going to be doing the presentation. Somewhat shocked and horrified by the news, he needed a little bit of calming down.

The thing that calmed him down was knowledge they had imparted before. They simply told him to remember two things. First, that every single person in the room was intensely interested in what he had to say. And second, that he should remember that he knew far more about his subject than any of the people he was presenting to.

# CHAPTER 15

# Magic, theatre, genius and other myths about pitching

Pitching is often seen as a black art – and good pitchers encourage this! It isn't. How, when and why to deploy techniques that will make you look brilliant.

The operative word in the title of this chapter is 'myths'. Pitching is often considered to be something of a black art, with words like 'magic' and 'genius' sometimes attached to particular individuals. Sometimes this is deserved, and there are examples of how a bit of theatre and magic can make the difference between an average pitch and a brilliant pitch. I would suggest to you, however, that prospects are not going to be swayed by theatre alone. Style alone does not usually triumph over substance. Much of what this book is about

> style alone does not usually triumph over substance

is the process by which the substance of the pitch can be made absolutely, uniquely fit for purpose. If you can achieve that then you are already a long way down the road to producing a brilliant pitch.

There are some tricks of the trade, but not all can be applied to every pitch situation. One famous character in the world of advertising was known for a particular technique of presenting creative work. He would have the piece of work in front of him so that he could look at it while talking over it. He would then do the 'big reveal' of the work to the audience. He would do so in very quiet, hushed tones. This had the effect of forcing the audience to lean in to hear what he was saying, with the side effect that they would concentrate very hard. A group of people all leaning into a table operates in a different way from a group in which the individuals are all sat back. It worked a treat. You can't do it with a big audience, but it works really well with smaller groups. If it is appropriate, you could consider trying this technique to punctuate the pitch and draw your audience into the key moments of the presentation. The standard advice is usually to speak up and speak clearly. It's not a rule. Experts will also tell you that in pitches people often talk too fast. This is true. I have seen it many times, and slowing down (even if it feels that you are talking too slowly) is something to work on.

## If you feel uncomfortable, you'll sound uncomfortable

The way you speak will, like it or not, be influenced by how nervous you feel. The following story from Rick Sareen, an ex-adman who is now in the agency coaching business (training, not bus driving), illustrates the random effects of nerves. One of the first pitches he ever did, as a junior advertising agency team member, was to the oil company Amoco. His role was very simple – he did the 'store check' and had gone out, taken some photos of filling stations, and had a mere three charts to present containing the findings. He had rehearsed thoroughly and frequently. On the day of the pitch his first mistake was to select a rather hot, woolly suit from the wardrobe. He stood up to present at the appointed time and soon noticed that his body was beginning to sweat profusely. So much so that he could feel his glasses slipping down his nose. 'It got to the point where I could hear myself talking,' he recalls, 'but I wasn't at all sure that what I was saying was what I was *meant* to be saying. I had to just stop, and hand over. It was hugely embarrassing.' He wasn't the first and certainly won't be the last person to find his physiology taking over at the wrong time. It wasn't a lack of rehearsal that was to blame, simply a poor choice of suit, which made him too hot and exacerbated the nerves. It's that simple. The inherent nervousness we all feel, especially in the early stages of a career, can be helped by simply making yourself feel as physically comfortable as you can.

 **tip**

Pitching is hard. Do yourself a favour and make sure that on the day, whatever you may be feeling, you'll at least be feeling comfortable.

## Don't allow yourself to get overconfident

The flip side of nervousness – confidence – can be equally dangerous. A sales pitch was taking place to the main board of an international plc. There were only two on the pitch team, the salesperson plus a colleague he'd taken along to field any detailed technical questions. The sales guy continues the story: 'As the board members began to arrive my colleague took off his jacket to reveal a short-sleeved shirt. In an effort to build rapport I joked that if we won their business I would personally buy him a proper shirt with long sleeves and cufflinks. At that point the MD came into the room and took off his jacket. Yes – a short-sleeved shirt. I found it difficult to look him in the eye during the presentation.'

Over-confidence can cause little slips, which can in turn become major problems. Attention to detail often suffers when you are that little bit too sure of yourself. Having had a proposal accepted in concept by the board of a major prospect, a pitch leader was asked to give more detailed presentations to the directors of each major division involved. Next up was the finance

> attention to detail often suffers when you are that little bit too sure of yourself

division. During this pitch the deputy finance director stopped the presenter in mid-flow: 'Is there any reason that your cost figures don't add up?' Typically, the finance guy hadn't been listening to the pitch at all, but had been doing his sums instead. The net of that little slip was the entire decision was delayed by two months and the sales team had to resubmit the entire proposal with reworked costs and benefits.

Even the very best pitchers can occasionally get complacent. This is particularly likely to happen if your pitch is not a one-off, but a one-size-fits-all pitch such as a standard solution aimed at a particular industry sector. You will know by now that I don't believe in the concept of the one-size-fits-all pitch in any case, but this story illustrates a common problem. In this instance a sales executive was giving a round of high-level presentations to the heads of IT of the various clearing banks. It was a standard pitch announcing his company's new in-branch banking terminals. He had prepared and rehearsed his pitch to perfection and was on his feet in front of the third prospect – calm, confident and well on the way to closing a multimillion pound order. About halfway through the pitch he slowly began to realise that he had completely forgotten which bank he was presenting to. They all seemed the same. He began to look around the room as he was presenting for any clues. Very quickly he lost all his rhythm and began repeating himself. In the previous two pitches he had invited questions with confidence. 'That day I couldn't get out of the room fast enough!' he admits. It was only when leaving their offices, and handing back his visitor's pass at reception, that he noticed the black horse on a green background. If only he'd looked at it on the way in.

## A little enthusiasm goes a long way

At the other end of the scale, a highly *personalised* approach delivered with *enthusiasm* is a reliable formula for successful pitching. You can have the best content in the world, but if you sound like you're bored by it, don't expect anyone else to buy into it. Enthusiasm goes a long way. By 'enthusiasm', I do not mean that you should be *sounding* enthusiastic, I mean that you should *be* enthusiastic. Bill Hart, Chairman of integrated agency SOUK, has an illuminating story concerning a pitch to Massey Ferguson, the tractor manufacturer. It shows how people respond to enthusiasm, as well as how professional enthusiasm can deliver on the personal level. Whilst in the early research phase, the creative director had decided to conduct a little extra research of his own. It's all very well commissioning formal, set-piece research to explore particular audience types, but real people don't always show themselves in their true light in a formal set-piece environment, despite what the people who sell 'research methodologies' may tell you. As we know from particle physics, the very act of observation can in itself change the nature of the phenomenon being observed. So it is with people; there's no substitute for getting your information from the horse's mouth. Or in this case, the farmer's.

And so it came about that the creative director had the bright idea of inviting back some farmers from the local pub, for an extended piece of 'kitchen table' research. The well-known effect, noted by Pliny the Elder, of *in vino veritas* ('in wine is truth') – or, in this case, *in beer veritas* – generated a great deal of relevant material, much of which could be applied to the pitch in hand.

In the pitch rehearsal the team ended up agreeing that in the interests of brevity, this section would be cut right down to four minutes on the day.

Come the big day . . . you can probably guess what's coming. The creative director became so enthused with the stories that he overran his slot. By quite a margin. The team were nervous. In fact, on the way home on the train, they had concluded that they had done themselves justice in the pitch, but this was tempered by deep unease about busting the time constraints. Pretty much all of the extra time they had used was accounted for by the kitchen table storytelling. The happy ending is that they won the pitch, and the client made a point of telling them that they had been particularly impressed by the enormous enthusiasm demonstrated by the creative director and his kitchen table story.

What I like about this story is that it pulls together a number of themes from this book in one hit. There is the obvious research angle – and getting your homework right is always important. But it's not just that the content generated by the research is 'useful', it's also the fact that simply having it inside your head gives a great sense of confidence. You really do feel like you're on top of the subject, which helps you to be on the top of your game. But I think the greatest value of all was that it enabled the creative director to speak with passion, based on first-hand knowledge. It was that passion, I suspect, more than the content itself that helped carry the day. Yet again, we discover that people respond to people, and in the end people buy people. They always do.

> people respond to people, and in the end people buy people

## Think about the most appropriate communications tools

There is a well-used phrase in advertising: 'the medium is the message'. This is where the *delivery mechanism* in itself makes a significant contribution to the message you are trying to communicate. An equally well-worn illustration of this is the 'fresh eggs' story (there are now three or four versions of this – I'm not sure which one is the original – but the underlying principle remains the same). The general idea is to imagine yourself driving down a road at which point you pass a sign saying 'fresh eggs'. It's professionally made out of shiny plastic, probably back-lit by a fluorescent strip. A few yards further on is another sign saying 'fresh eggs' – only this one is handwritten in chalk, on a piece of wood nailed to a post. The suggestion is that the latter sign is the one that is more likely to convince you that these eggs really are fresh. Although the wording is exactly the same, the look and feel of the delivery mechanism conjures up mental images of clucking hens scratching round an old barn in a sun-dappled orchard ... So far so good. Now imagine the same delivery mechanism of handwritten chalk on rough-hewn wood, but with different words: 'flying lessons'. Suddenly the imagery – imagery created purely by the delivery mechanism, not the content – is completely counterproductive.

**brilliant tip**

PowerPoint is not the only communications tool. If you use standard ways of communicating, you shouldn't be surprised if you get standard results. A bit of creativity will help you stand out from the crowd.

In a pitch situation, similar thinking can and should be applied. Jeremy Garner, Creative Director of digital agency Weapon7, told me a story of a recent pitch. The prospects were the marketing representatives from a brand which considers itself to be all about 'authenticity'. A brand for real people in the real world, with a story that needed to be told in a manner consistent with that. Therefore, anything that looked like 'marketing' was to be avoided. The first thing they decided to do was dump the ubiquitous PowerPoint presentation as a delivery tool. I tend towards the view that the love of PowerPoint is the root of many evils, especially in marketing and sales, so I was keen to find out what they chose as the alternative. In fact, they decided to present the whole thing off a live blog. This immediately gave the proceedings a decidedly un-marketing-like atmosphere and turned the meeting into a much less formal event. Now, they could show off the thinking and the work in an authentic, relevant context. By choosing a delivery method that suited the client and the task, they were able to give themselves an edge over the competition from the outset. He feels it was a significant factor in helping them win the pitch and I feel sure he's right.

## Check your assumptions

A valuable tip for anyone involved in pitching is to ask yourself the question, 'I think that's the case ... but do I really *know* that?' This is because in order to join the pantheon of master pitchers, step one is to avoid cocking it up by making assumptions. It's easy to make assumptions, especially if you think a pitch situation is similar to one you have faced previously. A nice example of this comes from the world of technology. The person concerned had been invited by an association of computer specialists to present a review of some leading-edge technology projects. No problem with that, our hero thinks. Having done that many times, it was a familiar situation. The day arrived and he hurriedly picked up his laptop with the standard 12-slide presentation and dashed out of the door to the waiting taxi. He had assumed an audience of a dozen or so hard-core techies and 30 to 45 minutes at the most to give the pitch. And why not? That's how it had been on previous occasions. But he had not asked the question, 'But do I really *know* that?'

> avoid cocking it up by making assumptions

He was greeted by two gentlemen as he alighted from the taxi. They escorted him through the reception area and one of them asked him when he would like the coffee break, observing that it was usually taken halfway through the presentation – after an hour or so. Imagine his surprise (if that's the right word) when they pushed open the double doors to reveal an audience of some 250 sitting expectantly in the university's main lecture theatre.

## Think about the pitch environment

Given a choice, you would choose to pitch on your own turf rather than somewhere else. In your own location you can check that everything works (but then assume that it will have broken by the following morning, so have a back-up of everything). An agency that was hugely successful in the 1970s and 1980s, called Allen, Brady and Marsh, had an astonishing pitch record. They would rehearse down to the last little detail, orchestrating the seating plan, dressing the pitch environment, sometimes even to the extent of putting little pieces of tape down on the floor to indicate where the actors in this mini-drama were to stand.

You can also dress your location appropriately. Some agencies have gone to extraordinary lengths to impress clients in pitches through the way they dress the setting. They have taken entire windows out in order to get a car company's vehicles into their reception area, hired film props of aircraft cabin interiors to impress airline clients, turned their reception into a South Sea island beach and so on. Clients like that, although they rarely admit it. What impresses them is the sheer degree of *commitment* shown by the agency. Back to the 'people buy people' maxim. It is no surprise that pitches often get won by people who have *demonstrated* their level of desire and commitment. Pitches also get lost by people who don't seem to be as interested. One pitch was lost because the pitch team members had spent so much time taking notes in the pitch that they came across as not interested enough. As the prospect later remarked to one of his colleagues, in a pitch, you need to *take note, not notes.*

**CHAPTER 16**

# Masterclass: it doesn't get any better than this

A series of hints and anecdotes from great exponents of the art of pitching, and some who are on the receiving end. To enlighten and encourage!

It's obvious that we can all learn from the masters in any field, not just in pitching. The masters themselves, however, have learned too. They've learned from their mistakes. For this reason I intend to focus as much on what we can learn from the *mistakes* as from the successes. People who consistently win pitches tend to be people who consistently avoid making mistakes. As Woody Allen once said when asked the secret of his success, it's a case of 'keep turning up for the auditions'. A similar dogged persistence in the area of eliminating mistakes is arguably more valuable than the magic, theatre and genius.

## Pitching is a dialogue, not a monologue

The need to keep your audience engaged has been mentioned before. Avoid the temptation to get so wrapped up in what you know you want to say, that you fail to read the audience. The art of pitching is also the art of dialogue. A former colleague had spent a couple of weeks' hard work preparing a

> the art of pitching is also the art of dialogue

closing presentation. This was going to be the final pitch to close the sale; the contracts had even been sent over to the prospect and this was now the endgame. Nothing was going to stand in the way of him giving the pitch of his life. It was going to be brilliant.

The decision makers assembled and he started. He was good. In fact, he was very good. He noticed that the prospect's finance director wanted to say something but, not wanting to destroy the flow, he asked him to hold any questions to the end – some 30 minutes away. Thirty minutes or so later, he finished and turned to the finance director, inviting him to ask his question. 'At our board meeting this morning we signed the contract you sent over to us last week. I just thought you might want to know that!' In this case not a failure to read the audience, just a denial of the findings. Not a disaster, fortunately.

I wouldn't want you to assume that advertising pitches always go swimmingly well and invariably end up with Cristal champagne all round, following yet another triumph of the art of pitching. It's not like that. Things do go wrong, at all points in the process.

## Check the room

One pitch went wrong simply due to the room décor. This was reported to me by a witness from a large American digital agency 'who were great at talking a good game', but not so good at making sure the office was in good working order. One Christmas, they were busy working on a monumental pitch, the kind that keeps half the company there for several consecutive weekends. In a distracted moment before the pitch our witness noticed there was a strip of plastic jutting off the wall. 'I pointed it out, and someone half-heartedly put some sticky tape over it and went back to talking a good game.'

Come the day of the pitch and a 12-strong marketing team from a major telecommunications company enter the room. The pitch goes to plan. Finally, the clients file out of the room in a haze of handshaking, at which point the most senior client – a not unattractive lady in a dress – catches her leg on the jutting plastic, really hard. So hard it draws blood. Oh dear. All that good work undone in a moment.

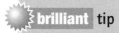 **tip**

A brilliant pitch deserves a brilliant venue. Think about your venue; what could possibly go wrong? (Be cautious.) Then take a step back and ask, 'What can we possibly do to make this venue brilliant?' (Be creative!)

## Dramatise the proposition

'Mistakes' can, however, be a deliberate part of a pitch strategy. The agency ABM famously pitched for the British Rail business back in the days when the service left a great deal to be desired. The clients duly turned up at the agency's office to hear what they had to say. The reception area was somewhat shabby, actually extremely so. The receptionist was busy manicuring her nails and completely ignored them when they came in. They spent some time sitting around waiting; no refreshments were offered and they had to take care not to get their elbows caught in the cigarette-butt filled ashtrays. A pitch seemingly about to turn into a train wreck. Except for the fact that, as was revealed with some dramatic value by the senior management of the agency, it had all been done to make a point. This, they pointed out, is how *you* treat *your* customers. It doesn't feel great, does it? Now we're going to tell you how to fix it.

## Any cloud can have a silver lining

Mistakes can also occasionally be salvaged and turned to your advantage. Dominic O'Meara, CEO of innovative Anglo-Dutch agency The Community, reminded me of a pitch

> mistakes can be salvaged and turned to your advantage

he was involved in for the Central Office of Information, for a campaign to combat car crime. The creative team had come up with an idea and decided to shoot a test film to show at the pitch. Good idea – and one which has paid off handsomely on many an occasion. They persuaded the young account manager on the pitch to let them use his beaten-up, ancient VW Golf as a prop. Absolute assurances were given about reimbursement in the massively unlikely event of any damage (even though the car was clearly on its last legs anyway). The lad agreed (the director being a personal friend) and handed over the keys. The director and creative team, plus drama student, made their way round to the back of the agency to find the car and set up the camera.

The director, now fired up and ready for a Cecil B. DeMille spectacular, decides that to get more realism the drama student should throw a house brick through the passenger side window and then break into the car. 'It's worth the sixty quid it'll cost to replace,' he points out to the worried creative team, adding, 'In fact you could buy the whole car for sixty quid.'

They prepare.

Just as the drama student has thrown the brick clean through the window an oldish couple appear and run over to the scene in fits of rage. It's never nice to hear old age pensioners swearing, is it? This pair were effing and blinding like a platoon of paratroopers. Wrong car. The account manager had for once in his life found a parking space in the agency car park. It became, however, a highly authentic portrayal of the real-life distress that can be caused by car crime!

## The seeds of success (and failure) get planted early on

Pitch disasters can sometimes be caused by events that occurred many months previously. An agency, which had been responsible for a campaign on behalf of the Financial Services Authority, found itself pitching to a private sector financial services client.

The FSA work had followed the pensions mis-selling scandal, and had been, shall we say, somewhat severe in its treatment of financial services companies. On pitch day, during the very initial stage of the pitch, it became apparent that this formed part of the agency's 'experience' within the sector. The client homed in on this immediately: '. . . so *you* did that campaign, did you?' was the immediate query. 'Yes, we did that,' was the reply. The client at this stage literally put his head in his hands, and with a slight rocking motion the head stayed in that position for a minute or two more. Finally, the head emerged and the mouth exclaimed, 'I am *beyond* angry!' The pitch itself continued for a further two hours. And yet neither party, I suspect, was in any doubt whatsoever about the eventual outcome from that moment onwards. Sometimes it's just better to cut your losses and simply say, 'I'll get my coat.'

**brilliant** tip

Think of the pitch itself not as a self-contained event. Instead, it should be the logical conclusion of an ongoing communications process that began much earlier.

Yet at other times, pitches can be *won* due to events that had occurred many months previously. Many years ago, the agency Lowe Howard-Spink was able to build its business with a major bank over a period of a couple of years, from a tiny initial project to taking control of the entire account, worth around £30 million – a very substantial sum at that time. The final pitch was against a very large incumbent agency. The key to victory was the way they had operated in the preceding 18 months. The LHS team had been specifically instructed to spend as much time at the client's offices as possible. Even if there was no good reason. Over time, gradually, they began to make friends around the office and they would chat about what was happening.

Sometimes, one of the clients might share that they were struggling with some problem or other (meaning, the other agency
was struggling with it) and this would provide an opportunity to
'take a look at it'. Eventually, LHS were able to force the issue
and suggest that they take on the whole business, and it went to
a pitch. A pitch they subsequently won. The time spent with the
client building and leveraging relationships did not merely get
them to that point, but had also been instrumental in securing
victory when the pitch came.

## Commitment is something best demonstrated

just because your pitch
is finished doesn't
mean it's over

It is not always the pitch itself that
proves decisive. Just because your
pitch is finished doesn't mean it's
over. There is still more to do. This
can range from seemingly trivial
things, which might make the prospect's life easier, to more strategic things that need to be addressed urgently on completion of
the pitch. Even the little things can make a difference, and their
worth shouldn't be underestimated. Rick Sareen, an agency
coach, told me the story of how a former colleague once had an
important group of prospects waiting for a taxi following a pitch.
There had been some hitch with the booking arrangements – no
cab. It was raining, and there would be a long wait before a
replacement taxi could arrive. As it was raining heavily, all the
black cabs that went past were occupied. The solution he came
up with was to stop an occupied cab waiting at the traffic lights,
bribe the occupant to get out and also bribe the driver to turn
round and pick up his clients. As any good customer service
specialist will tell you, every problem also presents an opportunity to impress, and the clients were certainly impressed by
this display of resourcefulness and commitment – qualities normally very hard to communicate to people who don't already
know you!

People do appreciate it when you go out of your way to accommodate them. One London-based agency had been trying with little success to get a pitch date in the diary with a prospective client. At the latest attempt, the client explained that while he would be in London that week, he had no spare time and would have to go straight back to Manchester on the train. Undeterred, the agency team bought themselves return tickets to Manchester and met with him on the train. The pitch went so well that they were able to get off at Stoke-on-Trent and head back with the business in the bag. I dare say the effort that went into securing the pitch opportunity had some bearing on the outcome.

## Watch the small details

Little details make a big difference, because people can react to things in unexpected ways – seemingly small things can mean the difference between success and failure. A marketing manager once attended a pitch accompanied by his boss, and they were ready to make a decision on the spot. They walked into the room and the boss said, 'So, no coffee and biscuits then . . .?' Blank looks on the faces of the pitch team. 'OK, I'll be off,' was the conclusion. The boss explained to his junior colleague that, in his opinion, if that was how they were going to start off the relationship then he felt there was no point in continuing with it.

## It's never over until it's over

Don't forget the big, important things either. The immediate aftermath of a pitch is an opportunity to regroup and address any important but unexpected issues that may have emerged. Your prospects may be wavering – perhaps they liked everything else, but . . . *Don't* leave any 'buts'. A follow-up call, email or letter can give you another chance to clarify, reconsider and, above all, close the deal. Prospects will not take this as a sign of weakness. In a world where everything is negotiable, do not be shy of continuing the negotiation. Many times I have seen victory snatched from the jaws of defeat, often by a last-minute offer straight to the top. An agency that specialises in below-the-line work 'won' a competitive pitch against similar agencies. At the death, the head of the client's above-the-line agency (which had been pitching for the advertising) called the senior client with a new proposal. If they were given the advertising work they would 'throw in' the below-the-line work for free. It was, to anyone in our industry, a ludicrous offer, but the client actually gave it serious consideration.

> post-pitch communication requires careful thought

Post-pitch communication requires careful thought. While it represents a chance to offer up some new alternative, I have also seen defeat snatched from the jaws of victory by overthinking a client's comments made during a pitch. Your proposal might have been, by comparison with your competitors, the one that stood out for being different, innovative, perhaps 'risky'. You may well have faced challenging questioning and some overt initial scepticism. But they may have warmed to it; they might quietly be coming round to your point of view. If you can discern any evidence that this may be the case, stick with your proposal. After all, if you don't have the courage of your own convictions, you can hardly expect your prospects to come along with you. Think hard about this as a team. If you believe your position is valid despite the prospect's reservations, go back and tell them that you have thought carefully about their position and want to reiterate your absolute conviction that your proposal is the right thing to do.

## Some things are best left unsaid (or at least unwritten)

If the date of the attack by Japan on Pearl Harbor is a date that will 'live in infamy', the 'spectacles' pitch to a major telecoms company must surely occupy a similar place in the pantheon of advertising agency war stories. This is an old story – it must be 20 years ago when I first heard it. It began innocently enough, with the agency presenting to the client in the traditional presentation room environment. The curious thing about this one is not what happened in the pitch but what happened afterwards. After the agency had been through, at some length, its full and exhaustive submission, the client decided as a body (there were a number of them in attendance) to make a request. Not an unreasonable one, by any means; they simply asked the agency to vacate the room so that they could confer amongst themselves and ponder upon the deep and wise thoughts the agency had put before them.

The agency took their leave. The conundrum of clients (I believe this to be the correct collective noun) remained in the room to deliberate. Left behind by the agency were various notes, printed documents and other pitch paraphernalia.

One in particular caught the attention of the client. This was a note that had been passed around earlier in the pitch. What could it be? Human nature being what it is (and, as you will have gathered by now, there is no pitch 'code of honour' that prevents such things), the clients uncrumpled the note to examine the contents.

The note read: 'WATCH THAT **** IN THE GLASSES. HE'S TROUBLE.'

As it happened, the chap (not the original noun used) in the glasses went on to occupy a role of significant seniority within the company. He must also have possessed not only a sense of humour, but also the ability to take a longer term view. There was a second round of the pitch. The agency was asked back. The entire client team turned up wearing glasses.

Once again we find we have learned something from a bunch of comedians.